JOYEUX
ANNIVAIRSINIRB
Luc x
PASCAL

Chocolat

Chocolat

The Art of the Chocolatier

TEXT
SERGE GLEIZES

RECIPES
VINCENT LEMAINS AND JULIEN CHRISTOPHE

PHOTOGRAPHY NOËLLE HOEPPE
DESIGN NELSON SEPULVEDA-OSORIO

SCRIPTUM EDITIONS

FOREWORD...

The universe of chocolate is a world of a thousand secrets, born of perseverance and passion-driven craftsmanship. Talking about chocolate is like talking about love; our emotions can be overwhelming. All of our senses are aroused: sight, touch, taste, smell …

Faithful followers of our brand know how passionate we get about the stories we tell, how we feel the need to dive deeply into each timeless universe. With *Les Marquis de Ladurée*, our newest exciting adventure, we hope to continue to develop our *savoir-faire*, but also to keep inventing and inspiring new emotions.

A devoted chocolate lover, M. David Holder, president of Ladurée, wanted to create a new collection that would, for the first time, shine the spotlight on Ladurée's chocolates, bringing these delectable morsels centre stage, to give the "food of the gods" its own moment in the sun.

With our new line of *Les Marquis* chocolates, we aim to add to our offering of gourmet delicacies, while preserving the elements that have been essential to our company's success: the perfect alchemy of beauty and goodness, an excellent product sumptuously staged alongside its own fine ingredients.

The indulgent act of biting into a piece of chocolate is, for some of us, an almost religious ritual. For others, it's a source of energy; for others yet, a drug. Given this all-consuming passion, we wanted to deftly unite compulsive food enthusiasts and thoughtful aesthetes, by opening a magic portal for both casual chocolate lovers and great connoisseurs into a dream world where the dainty and the delicious, the generous and the overwhelming, blend together wondrously in an entirely "chocolatey" universe. With *Les Marquis*, chocolate lovers will discover exclusive new collections of bonbons, pastries, baked desserts and of course macarons, all in a variety of chocolate flavours.

With *Les Marquis*, we wanted to cultivate the love of chocolate and the art of delicate confectionery. Without necessarily following modern trends, we wanted above all to pursue our quest for the ultimate indulgence, and establish the *Les Marquis* collection in the history of Ladurée.

Les Marquis chocolate pastries and bonbons are composed of a delicate balance of bitter and sweet, strong and smooth, melting and crunchy, foregrounding a plethora of gustatory aromas that find their source in flowers, spices, and fruits. From the traditional chocolate truffle to generous cakes and *financiers*, not to mention the indispensable chocolate bars, from the simplest to the most sophisticated, we've covered it all.

Contents

THE
ESSENCE
OF CHOCOLATE
PAGE 8

BONBONS AND
OTHER CHOCOLATE TREATS
TO MAKE AT HOME
PAGE 166

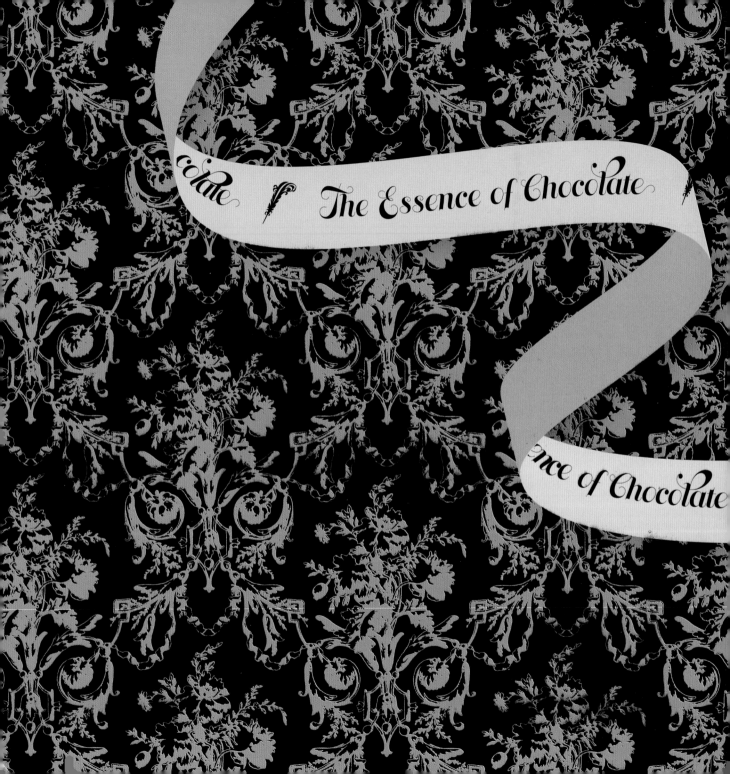

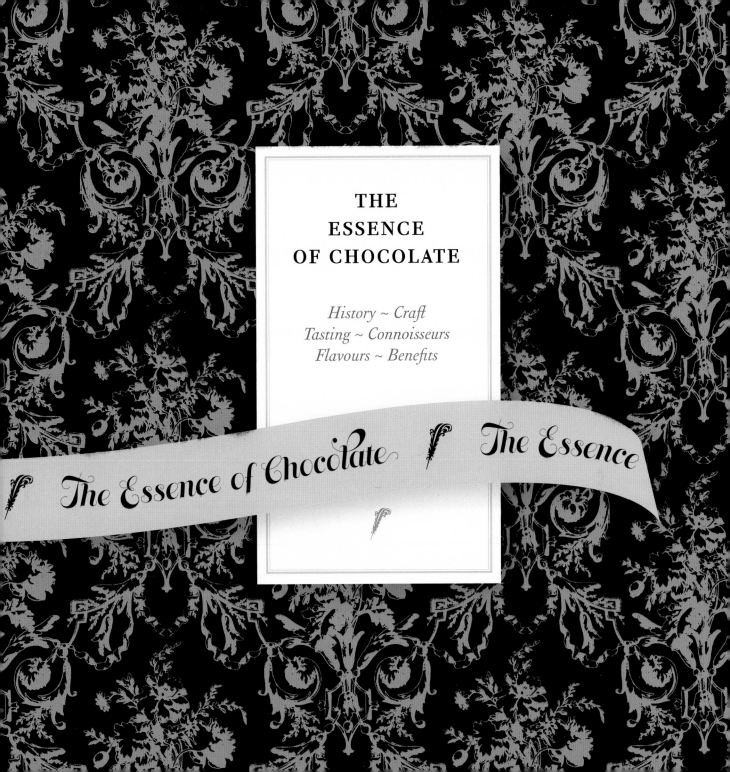

THE ESSENCE OF CHOCOLATE

History ~ Craft
Tasting ~ Connoisseurs
Flavours ~ Benefits

The Essence of Chocolate ~ The Essence

A BRIEF HISTORY OF

CHOCOLATE

From the foothills of the Andes to the courts of Europe:
the epic history of chocolate.

THE FOUNDERS OF THE GREAT HOUSES of chocolate were above all humanists, men of science and, without a doubt, children at heart. Jean Antoine Brutus Menier, Victor Auguste Poulain, Coenraad Johannes Van Houten... they were inventors, chemists, pharmacists, and each gave their name to chocolate creations that have now become global brands. Isn't it enough to say Debauve & Gallais, Suchard, Lindt or Nestlé, to evoke an air of divine sweetness? Through the nineteenth century, the courts of Europe were crazy for the bitterness of this funny brown beverage from the New World, whose virtues, before it was considered an indulgence, were above all therapeutic. An excellent antioxidant, chocolate was in fact understood to soothe stomach aches, and fight colds, fatigue and coughs. All this thanks to *theobroma cacao*, the scientific name for the cacao tree, the source of it all, the only tree in the world whose fruit grows on the bark and which produces *theobromine*, an alkaloid containing concentrated amounts of caffeine and theophylline. The etymology of the

FACING PAGE
Drawing of a cocoa pod, the fruit of a cocoa tree growing in Martinique or Guadeloupe.
CHARLES PLUMIER, 1688.

NEXT TWO PAGES
Left: Un-roasted cocoa beans from Santo Domingo Right: Bars of dark chocolate before being melted.

Le Cacao

name is quite revealing: *theo-*, for "god," and *broma* for "food." Chocolate truly is the "food of the gods."

AMERINDIAN ORIGINS

Chocolate was born on the other side of the planet, in southern Mexico and in Central America, and more specifically in the heart of the Aztec and Mayan civilizations. Its origins are told in a legend. After a fight with the princes of Xibalbal, the head of Hun Hunaphu, a Mayan hero, was hung from a tree. Instead of rotting, however, it gave birth the following season to funny oval-shaped fruits, cocoa pods containing seeds, or cocoa beans.

The word "chocolate" seems to have many different origins. For starters, some say it comes from the noun *xocolatl*, itself the combination of two words: *xocolli* (meaning "acidic" or "bitter") and *atl* ("water"), in nahuatl, a language spoken long ago in North and Central America. The beverage was already an important part of life's great moments, from birth to death, including marriage and childbirth. During these ceremonies, it was whisked up and served in liquid form to children as a means of purification. Since the drink was said to have been concocted by the goddess of Fertility, it was also distributed during weddings to ensure the fertility of the bride and groom. Even on the day of final rest, a chocolate drink was placed on the tomb of the deceased, as loved ones celebrated his departure by partaking of the same drink. In daily life, it would have accompanied certain types of fowl, like turkey, for example, in local recipes. One of the most famous Mexican recipes, still enjoyed today, is *mole poblano*. Invented in Puebla, in the seventeenth century, its spicy, cocoa-based sauce was enjoyed by princes. The less wealthy mixed cocoa with grits, to make a kind of purée, to which they added vanilla, anise,

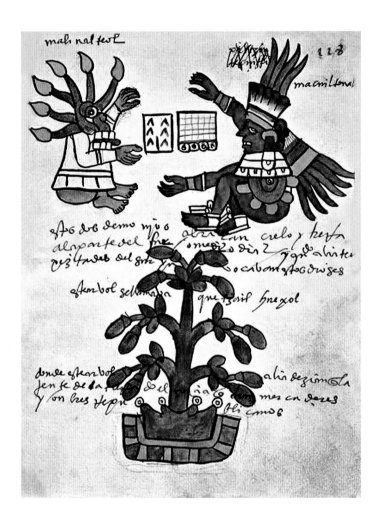

CACAO TREE

Illustration of a cacao, or cocoa tree, from an Aztec codex, annotated with explanations in Castillan Spanish, showing the extent to which local Amerindian populations were interested in chocolate.

TUDELA CODEX, 1553.

COCOA BEAN

This Mayan statuette wearing a cocoa bean on its waist was in fact a very elaborate container lid.

TERRA COTTA, CIRCA 600-900.

"The cocoa bean is a phenomenon, for nowhere else has nature concentrated such a wealth of valuable nourishment in so small a fruit."

ALEXANDER VON HUMBOLDT (1769–1859)

cinnamon, pepper, and annatto, a natural colouring agent used to offset the bitterness.

More concretely, chocolate comes from a magic seed, the cocoa bean, which grows on a tree with small evergreen leaves that shares its name: the cocoa tree. The oldest cocoa bean ever documented was in the year 1400 B.C. Cultivated for three thousand years, these trees, which grow up to ten to sixteen yards tall, produce pretty pinkish-white flowers and fruit in the form of cocoa pods. Originally, they grew primarily in the Amazon's Orinoco basin, in the foothills of the Andes. Today, they are cultivated in many other countries around the world, including Africa and Indonesia. Once they are harvested, dried, fermented, and roasted, the seeds of these pods become cocoa, or *cacao*, and are later turned into chocolate. The bean itself was so precious that it was even used as a token of exchange by Pre-Colombian civilizations, and by the Aztecs, in particular. In the sixteenth century, it was a means of paying for foodstuffs, debts, and taxes... One thousand two hundred beans were equal to one Mexican peso. A turkey cost a hundred beans; an avocado, three beans.

From South America to Europe

Until the sixteenth century, chocolate was still a misunderstood food in Europe, a drink consumed principally by the Indians and the Spanish of South America, who drank it hot or cold, topped with a layer of foam. They enjoyed it at the beginning of a meal, or at the end, as a *digestif*, blended with spices, honey, cane sugar, musk or orange flower water.

In 1502, Christopher Columbus had his first taste of the beverage on the island of Guanaja, in the Caribbean Sea, on his fourth and final trans-Atlantic voyage. In fact, several years earlier, in 1492, when he first set foot on American soil, thinking he had landed on the Indian subcontinent,

AMERICAN

This engraving shows an "American with his chocolate pot and cup, a cocoa tree branch, and some vanilla beans."

NEW AND INTERESTING TREATISES ON COFFEE, TEA, AND CHOCOLATE, PHILIPPE SYLVESTRE DUFOUR, 1685.

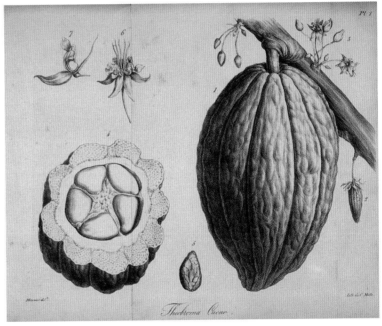

BOTANY

Botanical illustration of Theobroma cacao. *The cocoa tree is a small, evergreen tree of the Sterculiaceae family.*

MONOGRAPH ON CACAO, OR THE CHOCOLATE LOVER'S MANUEL, A. GALLAIS, 1827.

Engraving from New and Interesting Treatises on Coffee, Tea, and Chocolate. Philippe Sylvestre Dufour, 1685.

Tab.392.

Theobroma Cacao. L.

Lithograph representing the leaves and pods of the cocoa tree, from Icones Plantarum Medicinalium. JOHANNES ZORN, 1796.

FERDINANDO CORTES
CAVATO DA VN ORIGINALE FATTO INAZI
CH EI SI PORTASSI ALLA CONQVISTA DEL MESSICO

Amerindians had offered him cocoa beans, which he promptly threw overboard, mistaking them for goat droppings. Later, in the sixteenth century, Hernando Cortez, having returned to Spain, brought some of the chocolate drink to Charles V. The aristocracy, clergy, and Spanish colonies like the Netherlands, immediately went crazy for the new beverage. In response to growing demand, labourers were recruited in Africa, and slaves were brought by the boatful to work the cane sugar and cocoa fields of South America.

Chocolate arrived in France in 1609, with the immigration of Jews who, fleeing the Spanish Inquisition, sought refuge in the Basque region. It became so fashionable that it was even served in 1615 at the marriage of Anne of Austria and Louis XIII in Bayonne. Another fan of the drink, Maria Teresa of Austria, married to Louis XIV, then brought it to Versailles. The Court revelled in it, drinking it mostly hot, as they would coffee. Nobles and *gens de lettres* also took to the substance. The Marquise de Sévigné, for example, delightfully succumbed to its charming blend of bitter and sweet. She wrote: "Chocolate is flattering for a while, then it brings on a continuous fever..." After the aristocracy, it was the Church's turn to get into the act, to determine if this new substance which procured so much pleasure was not indeed a trampoline for debauchery, especially during Lent when fasting and abstinence were mandatory. After studying its composition, Cardinal Francisco Maria Brancaccio rendered his verdict, decreeing that chocolate was lean and absolutely did not interfere with the observance of the rule. And everyone breathed a sigh of relief...

Widespread consumption of this divine "soft drug" began, however, in England, where it was easier to purchase chocolate than in France and, above all, less costly. Several years later, all of the country's apothecaries were selling a new beverage concocted by Dr. Hans Sloane, made of a blend of chocolate and milk, which boasted therapeutic virtues. These were confirmed by the Frenchman Nicolas de Blégny, who, in 1662,

This Mayan vase was used for drinking spiced chocolate during processions of lords paying homage to their sovereign.
PAINTED TERRA COTTA, GUATEMALA, CIRCA 600-900.

published a work extolling the benefits of tea, coffee, and chocolate, for the preservation of health and as a cure for multiple diseases.

↳ THE TURBULENCE OF INDUSTRIALIZATION ↴

By 1780, chocolate production had begun to expand in Europe, following the invention of new machines designed to extract cocoa butter from the bean. A first chocolate paste factory had already opened its doors in Bristol. Its founder, Joseph Storrs Fry, supplied drug stores and pharmacies, once again confirming the therapeutic virtues of this sweet treat. His son continued the venture, increasing production with the first steam-powered cocoa bean grinder. Moreover, since 1814, cocoa tree cultivation had expanded in Africa, in particular on the Island of Sao Tomé, nicknamed "Chocolate Island." The growing number of factories and means of production thus made chocolate less expensive and more available to a wider population. Before then, the raw material had been too costly for large scale consumption. Bonbons, candies and cakes now emerged to fill the shelves of candy makers. In 1824, John Cadbury built a new factory in Birmingham (three years earlier, the company had invented the first dark chocolate made for snacking). In 1847, Joseph, Richard and Francis Fry introduced the first real chocolate bar, made by pouring a paste of sugar, cocoa butter and powdered chocolate into moulds. With this new discovery, which they presented at the Birmingham fair in 1849, the house of J. S. Fry and Sons became one of the premier chocolate manufacturers in the world.

In the nineteenth century, factories began to open in France, Switzerland, Belgium and Spain. With its green pastures and livestock, Switzerland would become the number one producer of chocolate in the first half of the twentieth century, before bowing to the dominance of the

FACING PAGE
A roving salesman of water, liqueurs, and chocolate, showing the era's passion for imported beverages.
COPPER ENGRAVING, 1695.

NEXT TWO PAGES
Left: Still Life of a Chocolate Service.
OIL ON CANVAS, LUIS EGIDIO MELENDEZ, 1770.

Right: Pieces of chocolate-coated candied ginger Les Marquis de Ladurée.

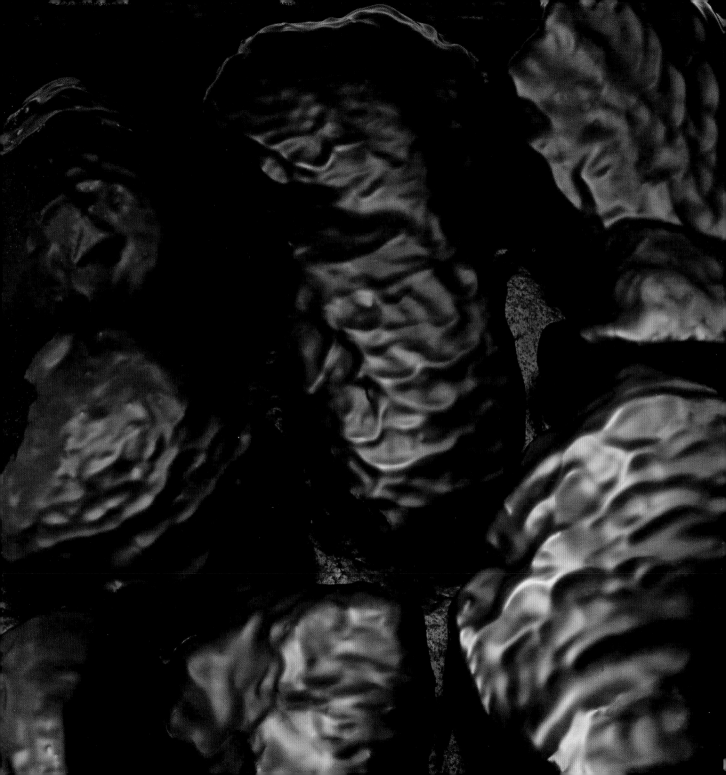

CORTEZ

When Hernando Cortés discovered Mexico, he was offered chocolate, which he brought back to Spain for Charles V.

RICHELIEU

Monks imported chocolate to France and had some presented to the Cardinal de Richelieu to regulate the healthy functioning of his spleen.

ILLUSTRATIONS, *L'ENCYCLOPÉDIE GLUCK*, 1904.

LOUIS XV

Courtesans watched Louis XV rise from bed, an experience known as "being admitted to His Royal Highness's chocolate."

United States (where James Baker had started his own company in 1780). In France, Jules Pares founded his company in 1814 near Perpignan, and in 1872, had a new, more modern factory built in Arles-sur-Tech. Originally from Vevey, François-Louis Cailler, who had discovered chocolate at a fair in Torino, Italy, lay the first stones of his enterprise in 1819 and would later build the first modern chocolate factory in an old mill, in the town called En Copet. Philippe Suchard had a similar trajectory, starting out in confectionery before founding his company in Serrières in 1826. With a passion for challenges of any kind, he also had his own steamboat built. *L'Industriel* launched in 1834 on Neuchâtel Lake. Three years later, he founded the first Swiss silkworm industry.

While hazelnut chocolate was concocted in Lausanne in 1830 by Charles-Amédée Kohler and son, the first "light" chocolate was invented in 1828 in the Netherlands by Coenraad Johannes Van Houten, who had developed a recipe with a lower fat content. It was revolutionary. He had thrown himself into his chocolate adventures several years earlier, in 1815, as a way of continuing the work of his father, who had opened a chocolate factory in the town of Weesp. By adding potassium and sodium carbonate to the mix, the latter blended easily with water and milk. Likewise, he succeeded in transforming cocoa butter into a powder, using a hydraulic press that he had also perfected. A true pioneer in the field, Coenraad Johannes Van Houten was the first to make filmed advertisements exalting the merits of his confectionery.

In 1870, a worthy successor to his father, Antoine Brutus Menier (he had invented in France, in 1836, the first chocolate bar mould), Emile Menier built his factory in Noisiel, in the Seine-et-Marne region. En 1876, Daniel Peter invented the first milk chocolate, using powdered milk. Three years later, he would meet Henri Nestlé, inventor of concentrated milk and later of white chocolate. The recipe for smooth, meltable chocolate appeared in 1879, thanks to Rodolphe Lindt, who invented the conching process, a new technique for refining cocoa, which consists in stirring the paste for a longer time, in order to render it as unctuous as possible, much like the process of churning cream to make butter. In 1899, Jean Tobler introduced the legendary Toblerone, with its base of chocolate, nougat, honey, almonds and egg whites. At the same moment, Philippe Suchard created the Milka bar. From 1900 on, new inventions appeared all over the world. The first chocolate-flavoured bars were developed by the Swiss firm Kwatta. The famous Mars bar was introduced in the United States, and the Nuts bar with hazelnuts by the Victoria company, which no longer exists, but which was once established in Belgium, the Netherlands and France. Invented to reduce cocoa butter content, white chocolate was born in the Nestlé workshops in 1930. Since its discovery in the seventeenth century, chocolate has never known a downturn and continues to expand into new markets, particularly in moments of economic crisis, when it emerges as an excellent antidote for the blues.

FACING PAGE
Painting: A Lady in a Garden taking Coffee with some Children, or The Cup of Chocolate. OIL ON CANVAS, NICOLAS LANCRET, 1742.

THE ART OF
MAKING
CHOCOLATE

*From the plantation to the chocolate factory,
to chocolate lovers around the world…*

From bean to bar, the process of making chocolate involves multiple stages: pod splitting, fermentation, roasting, grinding, tempering, and moulding. These manual and mechanical techniques haven't changed since the nineteenth century, since the industrialization of cocoa. The fruit of a tree cultivated in exotic countries, chocolate has always been produced using the same gestures and the same alchemy, a blend of heat and rest, of simultaneous passages through darkness and light, of precise proportions and a dash of poetry.

CHOCOLATE'S "GRANDS CRUS"

At the heart of the matter is the cocoa bean, nestled in its protective pod, the oblong seed that grows on the bark of the cocoa tree and is

FACING PAGE
Marquis Camées
in dark chocolate.

NEXT TWO PAGES
*A cocoa plantation
in the Caribbean.*
OIL ON CANVAS,
ALEXANDRE SOLDE,
1822-1893.

PAGES 42-43
*Left: A fresh
cocoa pod.
Right: A teaspoonful
of cocoa powder.*

VENEZUELA

Cocoa harvest in Venezuela. Illustration published in a chapter entitled "Everything About Cacao."

HISTORICUS, 1892.

N.º 1. Récolte du Cacao.

COCOA HARVEST

The cocoa harvest, illustrated in The Industrial Gallery or Application of Natural Products to Arts and Crafts in France and its Colonies.

ANONYMOUS LITHOGRAPH, 1825.

harvested twice a year. Particular care is taken with these trees, which are monitored with an attentive eye so as to prune unnecessary *chupons*, parasitic branches that grow on the trunks and feed on the plant's reserves, depriving the pods of the nutrients needed for their development. Growing in the warmer regions of the globe, cocoa trees exist in many different varieties, of which we will note three principal ones. First, the *criollos*, the rarest, constituting only a tiny percentage of world production. Originally grown in Venezuela, they are now cultivated in Mexico, Central America, Colombia and Madagascar. Their beans are fragile, with a very thin skin; their cocoa has a beautiful pastel colour. The *forasteros*, on the other hand, represent the greatest share of global production. Originally grown in the Amazon, they are now cultivated in central Africa, Brazil and Ecuador. Their lovely yellow pods each enclose about forty beans. Finally, the *trinitarios*, a hybrid of the first two varieties, were bred in the seventeenth century on the island of Trinidad and are cultivated today in Cameroon and in Asia. Other varieties of cocoa trees exist, like the *cupuaçu*, which principally grows in Brazil and is the source of the chocolate shape called the "cupulate."

SUNNING, DRYING, AND ROASTING

Once ripe, the pods change colour, some taking on a delicate plum-like hue, others turning slightly orange. After harvesting, they are split in half, freeing their precious beans. Once separated from their matrix, the latter are left to rest in containers covered with banana leaves, creating a kind of steam oven where the ambient heat reaches 40-50°C (105-120°F). After a week-long siesta, punctuated by frequent mixing, come the phases of fermentation – three total – at the end of which the beans are separated from their mucilage, a kind of white pulp, a process which causes them

*"What use are cartridges
in battle?
I always carry
chocolate instead."*

GEORGE BERNARD SHAW (1856–1950)

FACING PAGE

George Bernard Shaw, Irish writer.

PHOTOGRAPH CIRCA 1895.

to lose their bitterness. The first phase of fermentation, identical to that undergone by grapes after being picked and gathered into containers, is "alcoholic," transforming the sugars into ethyl alcohol. The second phase, lactic fermentation, transforms this alcohol into a new acid, which preserves the cocoa content. Finally, acetic fermentation gives the beans, which start out white or violet, their beautiful purple colour.

To reduce the amount of water in the cocoa, which is still high at this point (60%), the beans are again left to dry in the sun for two weeks, over the course of which they are rotated for hours, thus browning the beans uniformly and giving them a smoky aroma. Because they are fragile and in constant danger of being overly burnt, they then go back into the shade, before going back into the sun one last time. A final drying phase guarantees their resistance to transport as they are piled on boats and sent off to Europe's best chocolate factories in Brussels and Bruges, but also in Switzerland, England, Italy, Spain and France.

Fermentation and drying are two more important stages in the transformation of the bean into cocoa, as they contribute to the development of aromas. Once they arrive at port, the beans are roasted for forty minutes at 140°C (285°F). This process, which dehydrates them further, also optimizes their aroma, sometimes giving them that characteristic, slightly grilled flavour. The beans are then crushed, and the shells separated from the nibs, which are heat ground, transforming them into a paste, a mass of cocoa which liquefies at 100°C (210°F). This paste thus becomes cocoa liqueur, which can in turn be pressed into cocoa butter. After another round of grinding, the residue gives us cocoa powder.

FACING PAGE
A 19th-century chocolate factory. JEAN-CHARLES DEVELLY, 1783-1862.

NEXT TWO PAGES
Left: Crushed cocoa beans, or nibs, which are then roasted before being transformed into chocolate.
Right: Chocolate Mousse.

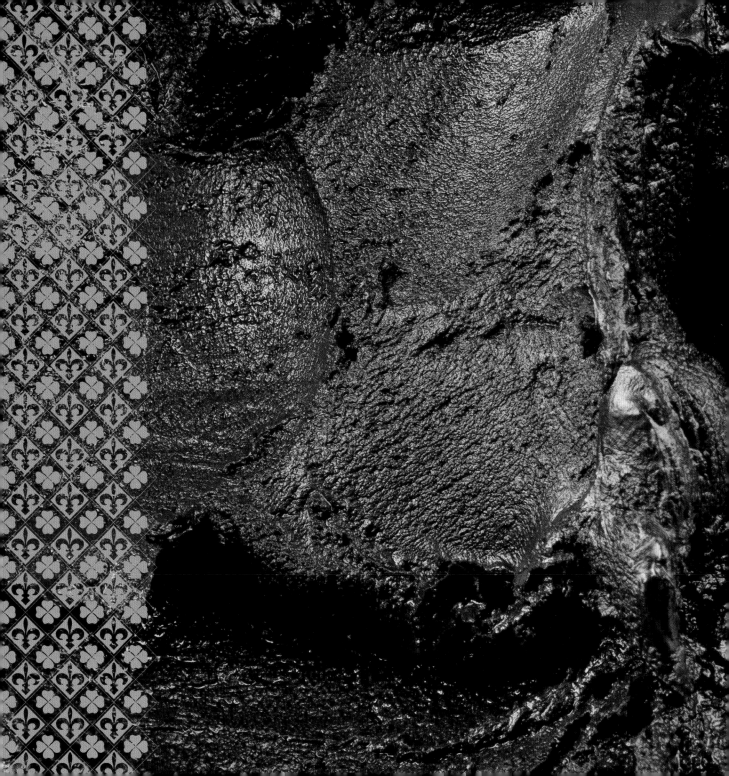

⤝ *Colourful Flavours* ⤞

Yet the raw material would never have turned heads, had it remained in its original state. Without the addition of certain elements of preparation, without the help of certain aromas, spices, most often vanilla and sugar, which serve to augment or diminish the cocoa content, this dark, aromatic paste would never have become dark chocolate, milk chocolate, or white chocolate.

Is it dark chocolate you want? Nothing could be simpler. Just add sugar to the cocoa paste. 35% cocoa is the minimum required to be called dark chocolate. For use in pastry, cocoa content is usually 65%. Beyond that, it can still be used in cooking, but is mostly appreciated on its own. Over 80%, the bitterness of the chocolate often limits its use to homeopathic treatments. Milk chocolate is made by adding cocoa butter, powdered or concentrated milk, and sugar to the cocoa paste (at least 25% to 40%). For its part, white chocolate is made without cocoa, using only cocoa butter, sugar, and sometimes powdered milk. Because of its very fluid texture, pastry chefs often use white chocolate in coatings or frostings for cakes.

Another phase, conching, consists in heating and stirring the enriched cocoa to make it as unctuous as possible. During this very slow mixing process, which lasts for about twelve hours at 70°C (160°F), soy lecithin is also added, to further homogenize the paste. In order to lower its temperature, the chocolate is then sent through tempering machines, where, at a constant 40°C (105°F), the chocolate crystallizes and can be worked and shaped, without turning white when it comes into contact with humidity. Once it has cooled, it will have the shine, firmness, and melting quality that we recognize. As for its shape, it depends, like cookie dough, on the moulds that are used. The moulding stage is when nuts, hazelnuts, or rice can be added.

PREVIOUS TWO PAGES
Left: Still Life with a Bowl of Chocolate, *or* Breakfast with Chocolate. FRANCISCO DE ZURBARÁN, 1598-1664.

Right: Les Marquis *dark chocolate and milk chocolate bars*

FACING PAGE
Top left: a cocoa roasting room.
Top right: a grinding workshop.
Bottom left: the moulding process.
Bottom right: the mixing room.
LITHOGRAPHS, 19TH CENTURY.

Aspirat Fortuna Labori

LA NAVE

FABRICA di CHIOCCOLATTA d'OGNI SORTE, di DOMENICO GUADO, IN CALLE LARGA à S: MARCO ALL' INSEGNA DELLA NAVE IN VENEZIA.

Prezzi della Chioccolatta
A Lire. 6. la libra.   A L. 5. la lib:
A L. 4. la lib: A L. 3:10. la lib:
A L. 3. la lib:

PREVIOUS TWO PAGES
Les Marquis *dark chocolate bars.*

FACING PAGE
Advertisement for a chocolate factory in Venice.
ANONYMOUS ENGRAVING, 18TH CENTURY.

The final phase. The sheet of chocolate then goes through a machine that vibrates, like a sieve filtering sand, spreading and settling the chocolate over the surface of the mould. Finally, as if to gather its composure after so much tumult, the preparation takes one last trip through a refrigerated tunnel to cool down.

Solid yet malleable, hard yet brittle, chocolate is an ideal medium for sculpting. It is often the focus of various pastry and confectionery competitions, like that of the *Meilleur ouvrier de France*, where the goal is to create a monumental piece of spectacular architecture – a church, building, monument, sculpture, a giant shoe or an edible dress – out of chocolate. These feats elevate the chocolate profession to the level of cheese, pastry, embroidery, or ornamentation, which each have their own high-level competition. Of increasing importance is the *Salon du chocolat*, which was started 18 years ago in Paris, and which now also takes place in many world capitals, like Tokyo, Zurich, Shanghai, New York, or even Salvador de Bahia.

And as with all beautiful stories, the cover is often just as important as the content. This is especially true at Ladurée, where the delicate box is part of the company's magical touch. Packaging has always been part of the creation of chocolate—silk paper, a box adorned with a famous painting, an old drawing, or a velvet ribbon. Chocolates are like precious stones offered in a jewel box that will be treasured like a wonderful memory, long after its contents are consumed.

FACING PAGE
Les Marquis de Ladurée *milk chocolate bars.*

NEXT TWO PAGES
Left: Still Life with Fruit and a Box of Fine Chocolate.
OIL ON CANVAS, 17ᵀᴴ CENTURY.

Right: Sheets of caramel with chocolate and nuts.

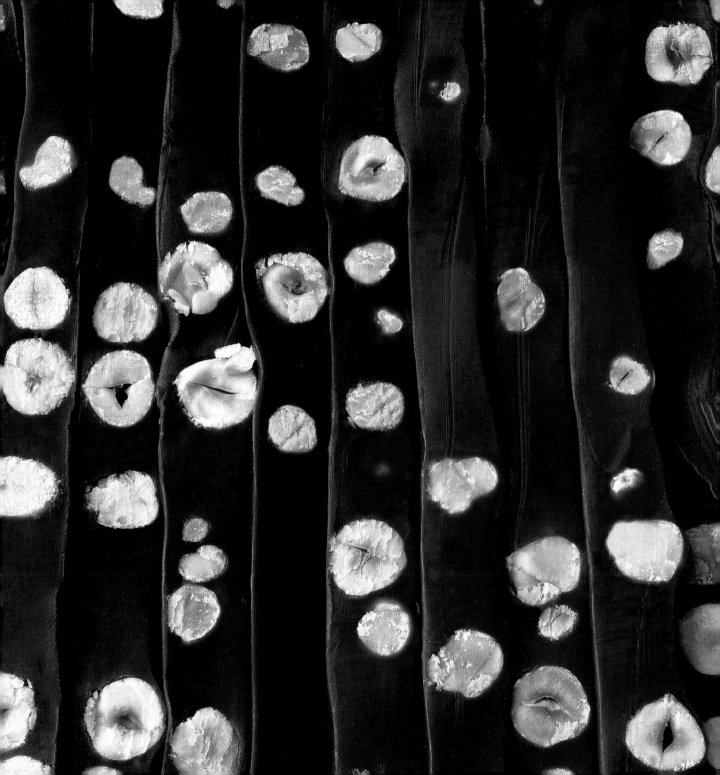

THE ART OF
TASTING
CHOCOLATE

Chocolate was once a novelty, an art de vivre,
with its own fashions and places of enjoyment.

CHOCOLATE WAS ENJOYED above all in the great courts of Europe, beginning in Spain, in the 16th century, when Hernando Cortez first brought cocoa beans back from the New World. A veritable food craze took over not just Madrid's high society, but the clergy as well, and monks in particular, whose monasteries became favoured places for enjoying chocolate. The phenomenon then spread across the borders of the Iberian peninsula into England. In London, the first chocolate shop opened its doors in 1657. France followed suit. It all began with Louis XIV according an exclusive privilege to David Chaillou in 1659. Originally from Toulouse, this Officer of the Queen obtained "permission to make, sell, and apportion a certain composition called 'chocolate,'" which he did out of a boutique on the rue de l'Arbre Sec, near Les Halles, in Paris. At Versailles, chocolate gained favour in every wing of the palace. The Queen was crazy about the drink and ordered her chocolate served "Spanish-style." Several years later, the divine beverage would be served in fashionable cafés, such

FACING PAGE
The Cup of Chocolate, *bringing together, in 1768, the Duke of Penthièvre, his son the Prince of Lamballe, the Princess of Lamballe and her daughter Mademoiselle of Penthièvre.* OIL ON CANVAS, JEAN-BAPTISTE CHARPENTIER LE VIEUX, 1728-1806.

NEXT TWO PAGES
Illuminating the ceiling of the Les Marquis de Ladurée *boutique, the grand, 19th-century Murano crystal chandelier comes from a Venetian palace.*

DRINKING CHOCOLATE

*Chocolate pot, moussoir, and long chocolate spoon
from the chocolate kit given by Louis XV to
the Queen Marie Leczinska.*

HENRI-NICOLAS COUSINET, CIRCA 1768.

le Clerc Inv.   *Barquey Sculp.*

Robe vraiment à l'Anglaise, sans garnitures, manches en Pagodes avec des Amadisses, le devant
de la Robe simplement retourné, formant un bord.

A Paris chez Esnauts et Rapilly. rue St Jacques à la Ville de Coutances. A. P. D. R.

as De Foy, Corazza, Mille-Colonnes, Lemblin, and especially the Café de Chartres, the future Grand Véfour. Located in the Palais Royal, one of the era's most in-vogue neighbourhoods, the Café de Chartres opened its doors in 1784. Customers loved this new place, decorated with woodwork and delicate *fixés-sous-verre* paintings, inspired by the four seasons. From the early morning hours, people would come to take their coffee or hot chocolate, served in one of those smoking chocolate pots emerging from the pantry, exhaling its delicious aroma.

⚘ THE CIRCLE OF CHOCOLATIÈRES ⚘

To enjoy this captivating mixture, which is taken very thick in Spain, France, England, and Italy, and more diluted in America, the great manufacturers of porcelain began creating *chocolatières*. Halfway between a teapot and a coffeepot, these chocolate pots were distinguished by their pierced lids, through which protruded a *moussoir*, a wooden stick meant to be rolled between one's palms in order to work the chocolate into a light, airy foam.

Chocolate services proliferated with some rather spectacular versions, like the one offered by Louis XV to his wife, Marie Leczinska, in 1729, for the birth of the *dauphin*, Louis Ferdinand. Baroque and poetic to the hilt, the set is the epitome of grace and femininity. For a while, the queen was known for being very religious and economical ("I don't need dresses when the poor have no shirts," she would say), and though she preferred to live in a large, private, less luxurious apartment at Versailles, she was nonetheless an accomplished aesthete, who liked music and painting, and even painted some ravishing little watercolours herself. In the space of ten years, she would give birth to ten children, only to be abandoned after her multiple pregnancies by her royal husband, who preferred the company of Madame de Pompadour, among others.

PAGE 66
Pyramids of Dark Chocolate and Berry Macarons decorating the Les Marquis *boutique on the rue de Castiglione in Paris.*

FACING PAGE
Series of porcelain cups and saucers made between 1772 and 1820.
MUSÉE ADRIEN-DUBOUCHÉ IN LIMOGES.

MARIE LECZINSKA'S SERVICE

Chocolate service given by Louis XV to his wife,
the Queen Marie Leczinska (1703-1768)
at the birth of the dauphin.

HENRI-NICOLAS COUSINET, CIRCA 1768.

At the age of thirty, the queen was already too weary, too old... She surrounded herself with things that would help her forget the pettiness of the Court and the escapades of her husband. Thus, the sumptuous chocolate service, which included not only a chocolate pot and its lid, but also a kit for making the chocolate oneself: a chafing dish for melting the cocoa and the milk, a mill for grinding the beans, a cruet for cream, some little boxes, a sieve, a sugar pincer, a candleholder, a bell, a big chocolate spoon, two small coffee spoons, and an ebony *moussoir*, not to mention a complementary service for tea or coffee. In homage to its illustrious owner, but above all to keep up with this era fascinated by luxury, it was made of precious materials, evidence also of the extreme attention now paid to chocolate: vermillion, porcelain from China, Japan, and Saxony, ebony, darkened wood and rosewood... The creator of this set, today on exhibit in the Louvre, was Henri-Nicolas Cousinet, master silversmith. Certain spoons are signed Christophe Blain. In keeping with the aesthetic criteria of the time, the decoration is burgeoning with flowers, reeds, palms, leaves, shells, stones and the dauphin's motif, in homage to the queen's first son, who finally arrived after his four older sisters. This service, which was kept in his grand study at Versailles, was left, at his death, to his companion, the Countess of Noailles.

The history of chocolate is so colourful that multiple museums around the world are dedicated to it, from Bruges, Cologne, Barcelona, and Prague, to Hershey, Pennsylvania, the American chocolate capital. Founded by Milton S. Hershey in 1900, the manufacturer owns a factory and a campus there, and has even named certain of the city streets after chocolate. Most notably, it invented Kisses, the famous bite-sized chocolates, in 1907. Other chocolate museums exist in South Korea, Mexico, and in Paris, where there is a museum that covers four thousand years of chocolate history.

PREVIOUS TWO PAGES
Display of silk ribbons for tying boxes of chocolate at Les Marquis de Ladurée.

FACING PAGE
Display case at the Les Marquis de Ladurée *boutique on the rue de Castiglione in Paris.*

NEXT TWO PAGES
Left: Cameo profile of a Marquis on the plaster wall decorated with acanthus leaves in the Les Marquis de Ladurée *boutique Right: Pyramid of Dark Chocolate Macarons.*

CHOCOLATIÈRE

*18ᵗʰ-century porcelain chocolate pot
decorated in gold palms and rinceaux.*

MUSÉE ADRIEN-DUBOUCHÉ IN LIMOGES.

⚜ LES MARQUIS, *THE REBIRTH OF A LEGEND* ⚜

The storefront was already there in 1934. *Marquis, le chocolat de Paris* had several locations throughout the capital: 39 boulevard des Capucines, 44 rue Vivienne, and 91 rue de Rivoli, among others. By taking over the name, Ladurée wanted not only to revive the legend of a company known for its chocolates, *dragées*, and other treats, but also to pay homage to an era dear to its heart, the 18th century. Of course, Ladurée had always made a special place for chocolates in its tea salons: upstairs, at its Champs-Elysées salon, for example, in a little private room whose walls are decorated in fine woodwork, but also on the ground floor of the Rue Bonaparte salon, Madeleine Castaing's old haunt. What was missing was a boutique entirely dedicated to chocolate, a place in keeping with the artistic style of its tea salons all over the world, which would provide a showcase for chocolate. It would be a new, precious and unique place to meet, through which the delicate melody of the Grand Siècle would continue to play, where one would come to indulge in sweet treats, of course, but also to experience an exceptional moment, an emotion, a feeling of wonderment, a return to childhood.

In the history of Ladurée's salons, where the containers, the jewel boxes, and the boutiques themselves have always been as significant as their contents, *Les Marquis* tells a new story, that of a refined Marquis of the 18th century, paying a courteous visit to the 20th century, having just descended from his carriage to bring a few sweets back to Versailles from the capital. This is the feeling one gets at the first boutique, located at 14, rue de Castiglione, under the elegant arcades between the Tuileries gardens and the Place Vendôme, among grand hotels and luxury boutiques, in the heart of historic Paris. From the street, the shop is distinguished by a black façade contrasting with the white, gray, and beige interior, with delicate touches of silver and steel. In order to create a space that both connects

FACING PAGE
A cavalier and a lady drinking chocolate.
ENGRAVING,
NICOLAS BONNART
AFTER ROBERT BONNART,
17TH CENTURY.

Un Caualier, Et vne Dame beuuant du Chocolat

Ce jeune Caualier, et cette belle Dame   Mais l'on voit dans leurs yeux vne si viue flame
Se regalent de Chocolat ;   Qu'on croit qu'il leur faudroit vn mets plus delicat.

VERSEUSE

Coffee pot with rinceaux decoration.

JEAN-FRANÇOIS GUILLEBERT, 18TH CENTURY.

CHOCOLATIÈRE

Still Life with Chocolate Pot.

MAURICE BOUDOT-LAMOTTE, 1901.

"I was unable to lift my mouth from the delicious edge of its cup. Chocolate to die for, thick, velvety, fragrant, exhilarating."

GUY DE MAUPASSANT (1850–1893)

FACING PAGE

Guy de Maupassant, French writer.

La Marchande de Coco.

à Paris, chez Ch. Bance, rue J.J. Rousseau, N.º 10.

Déposé à la Direction.

with its history and stands out from it, Ladurée designers played with new decorative codes and harmonious contrasts, bringing together history and modernity, while remaining as minimalist as possible. A concrete, milk-toned floor, Carrara marble counter, stucco walls, a ceiling illuminated by vertiginous Venetian chandeliers, which give the space an Italian touch... all come together to highlight their prize jewels, the chocolates, but also to render vibrant homage to the 18th century, that is, to beautiful works, to craftsmanship, to authenticity, to the work of passionate artisans for their art. Inspired by the panoramas of the time, the walls are covered with great white panels sculpted into acanthus leaves (the emblem of the century), made by *Auberlet*. The centre of these walls, worked as delicately as lace, is decorated with medallions, cameo profiles of various Marquis, which also adorn the Carrara marble counter, sculpted into drape-like folds. To make this counter, the marble was cut from 15-metre-long blocks and carved on-site by Italian sculptors. The rear of the counter is covered in sheets of steel, thus launching it into modernity. Perched on posts along the display case, small lamps light up *camées, bouchées, incomparables*, chocolate bars and squares, macarons, truffles, pastries, bonbons, and baked desserts. On the glass and brushed silver display shelves, designed like a bookshelf, are boxes, ribbons, chocolate jams... showing off their beautiful pastel tones. On the ceiling decorated with garlands and shadowy stucco, as if the flames of the candles had blackened them, great antique chandeliers, bought from a countess who was ridding her Venetian palace of its marvels, diffuse a diaphanous light throughout the shop.

PREVIOUS TWO PAGES
Left: The Chocolate Girl. PASTEL, JEAN-ÉTIENNE LIOTARD, CIRCA 1744.

Right: A cup of hot chocolate .

FACING PAGE
The Cocoa Merchant. LITHOGRAPH, ANTOINE CHARLES HORACE VERNET, 1758-1836.

NEXT TWO PAGES
Left: March – Downpours, April – Easter Eggs. ANONYMOUS LITHOGRAPH, CIRCA 1900.

Right: Dark Chocolate Easter Egg by Les Marquis de Ladurée.

MARS — LES GIBOULÉES

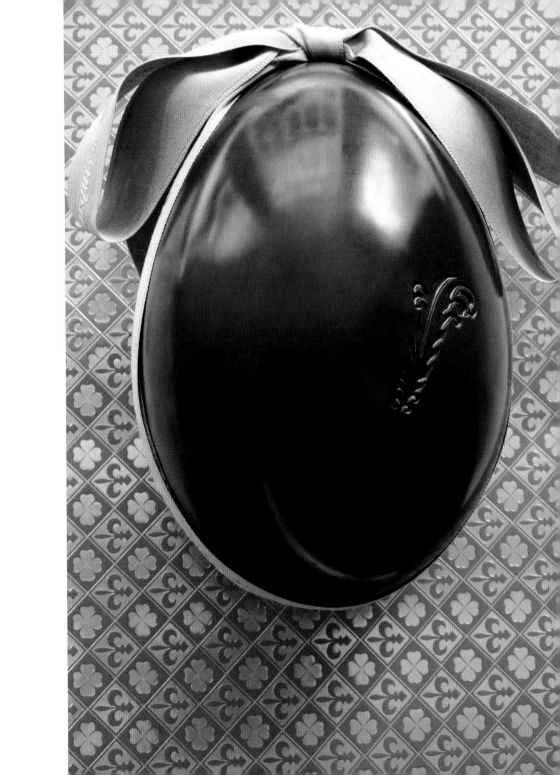

CHOCOLATE LOVERS

A CONSUMING PASSION

*Food lovers of yesterday and today – Marquis or not –
they're all crazy for chocolate!*

DID THE MARQUIS LIKE CHOCOLATE more than other aristocrats? At the very least, we know that the beverage, imported from the Americas, was very costly and was thus logically consumed in the courts of Europe. Anne of Austria, Spain's infante and queen of France and of Navarre from 1615 to 1643, apparently adored raw cocoa, that is, cocoa that has not been roasted, thus retaining its vitamins and minerals. To calm her changing humours, her daughter-in-law, Maria Theresa of Austria, would drink several cups a day, making herself sick in the process. Louis XV was also crazy about it and would make his own, in the kitchens of his private apartments, by heating an equal amount of chocolate and water in a *chocolatière* and adding the yolk of an egg. "Made the night before, it's even better," he noted in volume IV of *Les Soupers de la Cour* (*The Court's Suppers*) written in 1755 by Menon. Suffice it to say that the Countess du Barry, the king's favourite, loved this beverage, with its aphrodisiac side effects. Similarly seduced by the drink, Marie

FACING PAGE
Marie-Antoinette
*box of dark and
milk chocolate
squares filled with
tea-infused ganache.*

NEXT TWO PAGES
*Dark and milk
chocolate* Marquis
and Marquise
Camées, *filled
with rose-, violet-,
chestnut honey-,
and rum-flavoured
ganache.*

Antoinette brought to the Court her own chocolatier, who would add orange blossom flower or sweet almond to the mixture. Napoléon also liked to have some when he was at war.

⤛ FOOD LOVERS ON EVERY HORIZON ⤜

Globe-trotters eager for news of the New World were also understandably passionate about the precious bean. Alexander von Humboldt, for example, the German geographer and biologist, author of the celebrated five-volume *Kosmos*, published in 1845, had made several voyages to Latin America and completed various studies on botanical varieties, like the cocoa tree.

Good for the mind, chocolate also seduced men of letters. Philippe Sylvestre Dufour, for example, was a 17th century Lyon pharmacist and author of engraved plates and a treatise outlining the virtues of coffee, tea, and chocolate. Equally consumed with a passion for cocoa, Jean Anthelme Brillat-Savarin took a close interest in it in both his writing and his culinary preferences; he readily associated chocolate with love, stating simply, "Happy is chocolate, which, having travelled the world, meets death through the smiles of women, in delicious kisses, melting in their mouths." Politician, lawyer, deputy in the National Constituent Assembly, magistrate and above all gastronome, he was the author of many celebrated aphorisms and numerous books. Published in 1825, *The Physiology of Taste* made him famous. His chocolate addiction may have been the result of his exile in Switzerland, in Mondon, then Lausanne, after his deposition in 1792. "What is health? It is chocolate," confirmed this lover of chocolate in all its forms, "It is delectable in cream, and enlivens us again at the end of the evening, in ice cream and other salon sweets ..." Or again, "So let any man who has drunk too deeply of the

PREVIOUS TWO PAGES
Left: Silk ribbon and tissue paper from Les Marquis de Ladurée.
Right: Marie-Antoinette, Queen of France (1755-1793), brought her own chocolatier to the Court.
OIL ON CANVAS, ADOLF WERTMÜLLER, 1788.

FACING PAGE
Dark and Milk Chocolate Rochers.

*"Have some chocolate
so that your most unpleasant company
will seem good to you."*

LA MARQUISE DE SÉVIGNÉ (1626–1696)

FACING PAGE

Marie de Rabutin-Chantal, marquise de Sévigné.

OIL ON CANVAS, CLAUDE LEFEBVRE, 17TH CENTURY.

cup of pleasure, or given to work a notable portion of the time which should belong to sleep; who finds his wit temporarily losing its edge, the atmosphere humid, time dragging, and the air hard to breathe [...] let such a man administer to himself a good pint of ambered chocolate [...] and he will see wonders." In his books, we even find advice on how to prepare hot chocolate: "Monsieur, when you wish to drink good chocolate, have it made the day before in a porcelain coffee-pot, and left overnight: The night's rest concentrates it ..." Poet, novelist, playwright (*The Sorrows of Young Werther*) whose works have inspired operas (Gounod's Faust, Massenet's *Werther*...), a science, geology, botany, and optics enthusiast (*Theory of Colours*), Johann Wolfgang von Goethe was also seduced by the sweetness and bitterness of the chocolatey drink.

Undoubtedly, Marcel Proust also found in chocolate something to calm his spleen and his asthma attacks. The author of *In Search of Lost Time* also refers to chocolate in the first of its volumes, *Swann's Way*: "a chocolate cream, Francoise's personal inspiration and speciality would be laid before us, light and fleeting as an 'occasional' piece of music into which she had poured the whole of her talent." In a more intimate, but no less tender way, Colette would melt it on little spoons set on radiators, then offer them to her cats to lick. Chocolate also appears in a work by the Viennese composer Oscar Straus, taken from the play by George Bernard Shaw and adapted into English as *The Chocolate Soldier*. Transformed into a musical comedy poking fun at patriotism, it was a great success in London and Paris. The story is sweet and bitter at the same time: Raina, a Bulgarian, falls in love with a Serbian soldier who breaks down her door to avoid being killed. After confessing his Swiss origins, he confesses a passion for milk chocolate... a revelation that melts the heart of the young Bulgarian, who then forsakes her childhood sweetheart to marry the chocolate lover.

FACING PAGE
Box of eight Macaron Chocolates, *filled with dark or milk chocolate ganache, in different flavours: pure chocolate, maracuja-coconut, pistachio and rose.*

NEXT TWO PAGES
Left: Dark and Milk Chocolate Rocher *bites*
Right: Antoine Crozat, Marquis du Chastel, shown in full dress of Grand Treasurer of the Order of the Holy Spirit.
OIL ON CANVAS, ALEXIS SIMON BELLE, 1715.

ARTS OF THE TABLE

Series of coffee and chocolate cups and saucers in Sèvres porcelain (facing page) and Medici-shaped porcelain cup with twisted handle (above).

END-18TH CENTURY/EARLY 19TH CENTURY.

⨯ *NOBLE HEARTS AND RICH PASSIONS* ⤏

Certainly, when we speak of the Marquis or Marquises, we are talking about a world of refinement and excellence, to which chocolate, in its multiple aspects, naturally belongs. Bitter and acidic, sweet and salty, smooth or crunchy... chocolate has as many personalities as the Marquis and Marquises who each left their own unique mark on the century.

The Marquis were not all dilettante and spendthrift nobles who spent their time in luxurious laziness, collecting works of art, dressing in fine silks, feasting and multiplying their amorous conquests. Like those who came before them, even before the Middle Ages, most lived full lives as military men, economists, men of letters, or philosophers. At Versailles, Louis XIV and Louis XV readily bestowed the title on their numerous mistresses, the most famous of whom were the Marquises of Montespan, Maintenon and Pompadour. The title would be even more appreciated in the 19th century, during the Restoration, as a symbol of the Ancien Regime, in contrast with the redeemed nobility of the Empire, otherwise known as the "vanities."

Armand Charles Tuffin, Marquis de la Rouërie, for example, born in 1751, was one of the principle organizers of La Chouannerie, the Breton Royalist conspiracy which rose up against the ruling democratic power. Once a Trappist monk, nostalgic for the Ancien Régime, he left the order, fell in love with Mademoiselle Beaumesnil, with whom he had a son, then fled with General Rochambeau to America, where he became Colonel Armand. Upon returning to France, in 1791 he was part of the rise of the Chouannerie, a movement supported by the local nobility and the clergy.

There was also Nicolas Fouquet, Marquis de Belle-Ile, born in Paris in 1615, *procureur général* for the king, Superintendent of Finances, the most powerful man in France next to Mazarin. A lover of art, castles and beautiful women, he was also a patron of artists such as La Fontaine,

FACING PAGE
*Napoleon I
(1769-1821),
decorated with the
Iron Crown and the
Legion of Honour, a
great chocolate lover.*
OIL ON CANVAS,
CHARLES AUGUSTE
STEUBEN, 1812.

"… a chocolate cream, Francoise's personal inspiration and speciality would be laid before us, light and fleeting as an 'occasional' piece of music into which she had poured the whole of her talent …"

MARCEL PROUST (1871–1922)

P. Pauquet

OPPOSITE
*18ᵗʰ-century
Marquis.*
ENGRAVING, HIPPOLYTE
AND POLYDOR PAUQUET,
1865.

FACING PAGE
Boxes of chocolate,
Les Marquis de
Ladurée.

Molière, Poussin, Le Brun, and Le Vau, who designed his castle at Vaux-le-Vicomte. Louis XIV condemned him to life in prison for two reasons: for having courted his mistress, Mademoiselle de la Vallière, but mostly for having organized at his palace, in 1661, one of the grandest parties of the century, thus daring to tarnish the image of the monarchy. For the king, it was the straw that broke the camel's back.

Maréchal de France, the Marquis de Contades was named governor of Alsace in 1762. His celebrity comes from a famous dinner, where he asked his chef, Clause, to prepare some extraordinary dishes, among which was a *pâté de foie gras* which became famous around the world.

While the Marquis Henri Pascal de Rocheguide, military officer and man of letters with a passion for the Occitan language, led a discreet existence, quite the contrary was true of the famous Marquis (or Count, the debate continues) de Sade, condemned for his sulphurous works, which nonetheless have been part of the *Bibliothèque de la Pléiade* collection of classics since 1990.

Finding the title of Marquis rather superficial, after the 1789 revolution, Gilbert du Motier, the Marquis de Lafayette, began to sign his missives simply "Lafayette." Quite proud, on the contrary, of the title of General, this militant, pro-revolutionary politician, who would later also support the July Monarchy, made a name for himself above all by taking part in the American War of Independence. Ten years before his death, he had soil from the American continent brought to France in order to be buried in it after his death. The first man to free a slave, he even suggested to President Washington that he abolish slavery, in vain. His statue stands imposingly in front of the White House and his name has become that of a mountain, seven counties, and several dozen American towns.

A friend of Voltaire, Charles de la Villette, the Marquis de Villette, son of Pierre-Charles de Villette, seigneur of Plessis-Longueau and of Thérèse-Charlotte Cordier de Launay, aunt of the Marquis de Sade, was the author

FACING PAGE
Portrait of Louis XV, known for his tender addiction to chocolate...
OIL ON CANVAS, CARLE VAN LOO, 1705-1765.

NEXT TWO PAGES
Left: Box, ribbon, and tissue paper, Les Marquis de Ladurée.
Right: Sesame, pistachio, hazelnut, lemon, and crunchy hazelnut praline Pavés de la cour.

Horwood s.

OPPOSITE
*The Marquis de
Lafayette (1757–1834).*
ENGRAVING, CIRCA 1790.

FACING PAGE
Box of 14 Castiglione,
*filled with pure
Brazilian coffee-
flavoured dark ganache
and coffee-hazelnut
nougatine.*

of numerous pamphlets. Yet he stands out primarily for his love affairs with men and his liaisons with lesbians like Françoise Raucourt, member of the Comédie Française.

And the list would not be complete without Marie de Rabutin-Chantal, the Marquise de Sévigné. Her correspondence with her daughter, at a rate of about three letters a week for twenty-five years, was such that it was first clandestinely published in 1725, elevating the epistolary form to the status of literary work. In one of her final missives, she even advised her daughter to have some chocolate each time she found herself among unpleasant company, who would then "seem good," she said.

But France isn't the only country with distinguished nobility. Spain also had celebrated Marquis, as did Portugal, where the Marquis de Pombal, Sebastião de Carvalho e Melo, was a politician of great importance in the history of his country. Anti-clerical and decidedly abolitionist, he participated in the colonization of Brésil, thus encouraging cocoa cultivation, the growth of factories, and by extension the history of chocolate.

CHOCOLATE LOVERS OF TODAY

It is without a doubt the most appreciated gift in the world, one that we give at Christmas and at Easter, celebrations of birth and rebirth, of family, of the beginning of Spring, holidays that are definitively linked to chocolate. Valentine's Day, the celebration of love, is equally special, a day when, in Asia, young girls give chocolate to their fiancés. In Japan, a manga even tells the story of a heroine called Chocolate Girl. When it is not an edible statue, chocolate is also used as a balm for beauty and relaxation, leading beauty spas in the chic hotels of the Land of the Rising Sun to offer family cocoa baths. In Mexico, on 2 November, the Day of the Dead, hundreds

FACING PAGE
*Chocolate Nougat
from* Les Marquis
de Ladurée.

"Love chocolate completely, freely and without false shame; remember, 'there is no reasonable man without a spark of madness.'"

FRANÇOIS DE LA ROCHEFOUCAULD (1613–1680)

of little chocolate skulls are made to be set on tombstones, but also to be eaten. Otherwise, chocolate is most commonly found in the shape of bells, fish, baskets, chickens filled with little eggs... making each religious holiday a moment of indulgence. In ten years, chocolate consumption has increased considerably, with the precious cocoa bean becoming the third most coveted food stuff, after sugar and coffee.

Generally speaking, chocolate is most often purchased as a bar, whose squares are broken off and enjoyed between the tips of two fingers, in either homeopathic or gargantuan doses. We also love its liquid form, hot or diluted with water or milk. Some like it very milky, almost white, others as a kind of paste, dripping slowly into a porcelain cup.

A HISTORY OF RITUALS

Eating chocolate is above all a matter of ritual. Some eat it only at home, at a precise hour, at ten or four o'clock, in order to break up the morning or the afternoon, to fill an empty moment. One square, or two... (but no more, more would be a sin...) melting on the tongue, making the moment feel eternal. Others never eat it alone, not out of some grand spirit of generosity, simply out of a desire to feel less guilty and lure more accomplices into the divine sin. In this case, having only two squares makes no sense. And before you know it, the chocolate bar is quickly devoured.

In France, chocolate is intimately attached to our childhood memories. How can one forget our afternoon snacks, a slice of bread and four little squares of milk chocolate, wrapped in a paper napkin or a tissue, tucked into our school bags between a history text and a notebook? Bread and chocolate, punishment and paradise. Punishment being the bread, the thing one eats dry with water in jail; and chocolate, paradise, a reward for

FACING PAGE
Box of Pavés de la cour.

NEXT TWO PAGES
Left: Dark chocolate Marquis Camées *bites, filled with rum-flavoured ganache.*

a good deed. When the bell rang, a cruel dilemma presented itself. Which to eat first? The chocolate, then the bread? Or the reverse, to end on a high note? "No, both at the same time," the teacher would answer, putting an end to the torturous problem.

Another of our French "madeleines" is the *rocher*, that crunchy ball of milk chocolate. Being so filling, it was perfect for soothing sudden pangs of hunger, but mostly for breaking up the monotony of long car rides, or as a special treat in front of a Sunday night movie.

FACING PAGE
Les Marquis de Ladurée *Langues de chat, coated in dark and milk chocolate.*

GRACE & FLAVOUR

VARIETIES & VIRTUES OF CHOCOLATE

Bitter and sweet, smooth and crunchy,
chocolate is "the food of the gods"…

"THE UNIVERSE OF CHOCOLATE is a world of a thousand secrets […] Talking about chocolate is like talking about love; our emotions can be overwhelming. All of our senses are aroused: sight, touch, taste, smell …" Ladurée's message is clear. An almost religious ritual, a fuel, a drug… chocolate unleashes passions. To eat it is either a compulsion or an act of logic that leaves no one indifferent. For that matter, isn't there a club for Chocolate Eaters, like that of Tea Drinkers, whose job is to defend and share this common passion?

It's the same with everything chocolate has to offer: bitter or sweet, supple or strong, smooth or crunchy. These sensations emerge from aromas and ingredients that are added to it: flowers, spices, fruit, caramel… Uniqueness of flavour is often the result of contradictory impressions. There are even incongruous flavours, like those developed by chocolate makers in the Land of the Rising Sun, such as chestnut, Hokkaido squash, watermelon, sea urchin… In Japan, Nestlé has even created chocolate bars

FACING PAGE
Young Woman
Drinking
Chocolate.
OIL ON CANVAS,
FRANÇOIS DE TROY, 1723.

NEXT TWO PAGES
Left: Window of the
Les Marquis de
Ladurée *boutique*
on the rue de
Castiglione in Paris.
Right: Dark
Chocolate Bostock,
or Brioche, at
Les Marquis de
Ladurée.

"Any man who finds time dragging and the air hard to breathe should comfort himself with a hot chocolate…"

JEAN ANTHELME BRILLAT-SAVARIN (1755–1826)

FACING PAGE

*Jean Anthelme Brillat-Savarin,
French lawyer and gastronome.*

EAU-FORTE D'ALLAIS, AFTER LAMBERT, 1789.

flavoured with wasabi, soy, sweet potato or *matcha*, green tea. In Europe the flavours are more classic, and chocolate is readily blended with spices like cinnamon, cumin, ginger, anise, cardamom, sesame, pistachio, hazelnut, pepper, or mint. It's impossible to forget the famous "After Eight" chocolates, with their thin layer of mint cream in the centre, wrapped in shiny paper, a treat meant to be enjoyed after eight, we suppose, but which is just as likely to be munched on at any time of day.

SEEKERS OF SIMPLICITY

Paralleling this palette of exotic flavours, true chocolate lovers prefer simplicity, that is, dark or milk chocolate. Period. But this penchant for purity does not, on the other hand, rule out a desire for strong, clean tastes, for rich, contrasting textures.

At *Les Marquis*, we like chocolates that are strong in taste and in flavour, simultaneously light and aromatic, intense and dense, without being greasy, such that you could enjoy several at once without ever feeling like you've had too much. The result is a palette of nuanced, woodsy, spicy flavours, some with a berry base, a variety of chocolates created from a blend of beans from the Caribbean, Brazil and Madagascar. While, for now, the chocolate selection remains classic, new themes are surely on the horizon, as well as new collections reflecting seasons, stories, memories, countries, voyages…

FACING PAGE
Early Morning Chocolate, *a beverage whose virtues were also known in Venice…*
OIL ON CANVAS, PIETRO FALCA, KNOWN AS PIETRO LONGHI, 1702-1785.

OPPOSITE
Dark Chocolate
Corolle Feuilletée by
Les Marquis de
Ladurée.

FACING PAGE
Tissue paper and
silk ribbons at
Les Marquis de
Ladurée.

⟿ *BEANS OF HAPPINESS* ⟾

Where do the antidepressant, antioxidant, stimulating and addictive effects of chocolate come from? From what's inside. Rich in sugar and high in fat, cocoa is an excellent energy-booster, though not necessarily good for one's figure (which seems obvious, even though the regular consumption of dark chocolate, in reasonable quantities, doesn't always result in weight gain). It also contains caffeine, theophylline (found in tea leaves), which we also find in the famous theobromine (the "food of the gods"), vitamins A, B, D, E, etc., amino acids, as well as the famous phenylethylamine, a smart-sounding molecule which stimulates the production of dopamine, one of the "happiness hormones." Also rich in magnesium, phosphorus, potassium, iron, manganese and copper, chocolate is actually a marvellously healthy food. Certain nutrition guides even suggest consuming 100g (3½ oz) of milk chocolate per day, to provide our body with one-third of the recommended daily amount of magnesium. Cocoa's antioxidant and anti-inflammatory properties are also said to be good for blood circulation, thus helping to reduce hypertension.

Moreover, it was for all of these reasons that chocolate was sold in pharmacies in the 19th century. It has also been proven that it functions as a stimulant, giving us a little kick when we feel depleted, and would therefore, without exaggerating, be an excellent palliative for melancholia. It was even once said to be a bit of an aphrodisiac... One scientific study concluded that melting chocolate in one's mouth caused an increase in heart rate, and proved just as reassuring as a moment of shared tenderness between two people.

So is it addictive? Certainly, but no one seems to be complaining. This effect is assured by its stimulating, euphoric, regenerating, anti-stress molecules, but above all by the simple pleasure procured from a single square of chocolate, or by sharing this moment with a similarly passionate friend.

FACING PAGE
A caricature extolling the virtues of chocolate for healing the ills of the clergy.
ANONYMOUS ENGRAVING, 18TH CENTURY.

FACING PAGE
Window of the
Les Marquis de
Ladurée *boutique*
on the rue de
Castiglione in Paris.

OPPOSITE
Marquis *Dark*
Chocolate Savarin
with Grand Marnier.

Good for the heart, but also for the soul, chocolate is equally beneficial for the body, particularly when it comes to massage. European and Asian beauty institutes have demonstrated the virtues of cocoa for relaxation. Cocoa powder makes an excellent exfoliant, more so than an exfoliating glove, because less abrasive, and so much more tender... Mixed with shea butter, it transforms into a massage cream that regulates circulation, relaxes the body and mind, and leaves a luscious aroma on the skin.

⚘ CHOCOLATE: A DELICATE NECTAR ⚘

Like great wines, chocolates are classified by their place of origin. Today, these are found across South America, Asia, and Africa, which accounts for 70% of world production. Unfortunately, because they have not been well cared for as they age, today the cocoa trees of the African continent are in decline, and new plantations have been established in Vietnam, Indonesia (which as become the world's 3rd largest producer), and Madagascar (whose meagre production of barely 6,000 tons of cocoa per year is, nonetheless, of incomparable quality). In the northwest corner of the country, the beautiful, humid earth were the Sambirano River flows, is manna for the cocoa trees that grow on land blanketed in orchids and dried leaves. *Criollo* cocoa, the best in the world, the variety originally grown in Latin America, is cultivated here without pesticides. Another unique aspect of the island is its production of pods with hybrid flavours, the result of intense pollination, with the help of the smallest gnat in the world, gathering nectar from tree to tree.

When the cocoa comes from a single country, like the Fernando Po variety from equatorial Guinea, for example, French chocolatiers call these *chocolats d'origine*, or single-origin chocolates. We use the term *chocolats de cru* when the cocoa comes from a single plantation, like the Mangaro from

FACING PAGE
Dwarf offering a cup of chocolate to Doña Juana de Mendoza, future Duchess of Bejar.
OIL ON CANVAS, ALONZO SANCHEZ COELLO, 16TH CENTURY.

OPPOSITE
Les Marquis
Guanaja Chocolate
Eclair.

FACING PAGE
Detail of the plaster
wall at the
Les Marquis de
Ladurée *boutique*
on the rue de
Castiglione in Paris,
designed by
Auberlet.

Madagascar; finally, *grand cru* refers to cocoa coming from a big plantation, such as the Chuao plantation in Venezuela. Each of these unique sources gives the chocolate a particular flavour. *Forastero* beans from the cocoa trees in Ghana or Ecuador (the world's 2nd largest producer) have a toasted aroma. *Criollo* beans from Venezuela or Madagascar taste of spices, berries and tobacco. *Porcelana* beans from Venezuela, Peru, and Mexico, release flavours of warm milk and honey.

A WALTZ OF FLAVOURS

Chocolate tasting, for that matter, is a ritual nearly as complex as wine tasting. Like the aspect of nectar, a chocolate is first judged by its appearance, its colour, brilliance, texture, aroma, its smoothness or its imperfections. Another important element in its appraisal is the way it breaks, cleanly or softly, its way of melting in the mouth, of transforming into an unctuous, grainy, smooth or sticky paste. Then comes the waltz of flavours, its degree of bitterness, sugar, acidity, its more or less milky taste, to which extra ingredients are added: nuts, rice, or hazelnuts. In the final stage, its aroma diffuses throughout the mouth and into the nose, lingering in a more or less heavy or ethereal way once the square has been swallowed.

Ideally, chocolate should be eaten at a temperature of 20°C (68°F). Too hot, above 36°C (96.8°F), it melts; too cold, it turns white. When it goes through large temperature swings, when it ages, or when it is exposed to too much humidity, it becomes covered with a thin white film, a layer of fat or sugar, called "de-crystallization." To avoid this little unpleasantness, simply store your chocolate in a "chocolate cooler," a kind of refrigerator that will maintain the cocoa at a temperature between 14°C (57.2°F) and 20°C (68°F).

PREVIOUS TWO PAGES
Left: Pyramid of Orange Macarons filled with dark chocolate and Kalamansi juice ganache at the Les Marquis de Ladurée *boutique on the rue de Castiglione in Paris. Right: A chocolate bar in southern Germany or northern Italy.* OIL ON CANVAS, EUROPEAN SCHOOL, 18TH CENTURY.

FACING PAGE
Chocolate and Passion Fruit Marquise Religieuse.

"Whoever has drunk a cup of chocolate can endure a whole day's travel."

Johann Wolfgang von Goethe (1749–1832)

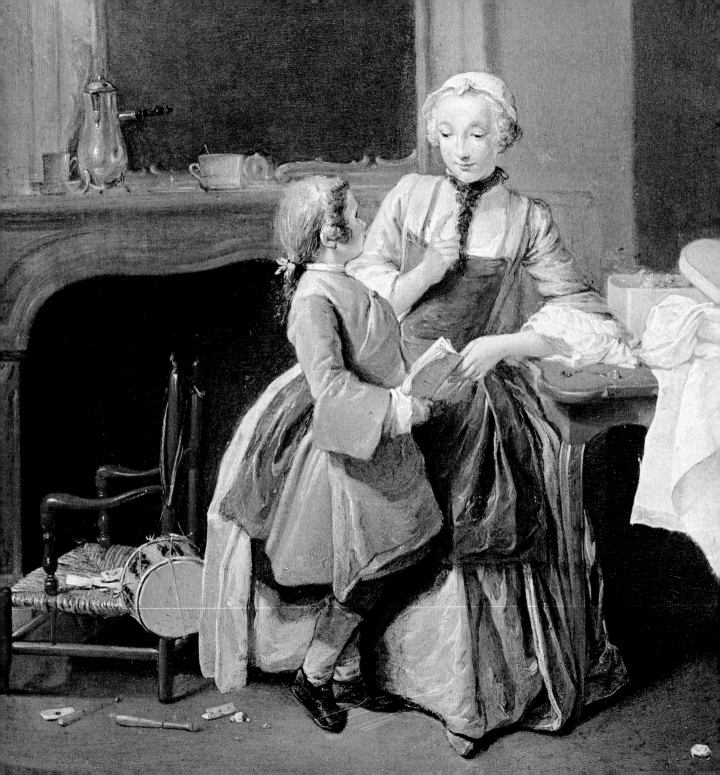

✄ THE ART OF SUBTLE COMBINATIONS ✄

Hardly shy of unusual pairings, and without overdoing it, chocolate goes very well with nuts, and with certain alcohols, like Chartreuse, for example, or Champagne. While true connoisseurs prefer their chocolate as is, others favour its liquid form, a warm sauce poured over vanilla ice cream, a pear, or *profiteroles*, a delectable source of vertiginous pleasure as hot meets cold, vanilla meets cocoa, and pastry meets cream! When chocolate arrives in the form of a light, creamy mousse, it is generally served with slices of candied orange rind, creating a sumptuous contrast with the acidity and crunch of the candied fruit. Other devotees take a square of chocolate with strongly spiced tea, as long as the chocolate is dark and contains at least 80% cocoa. Or with coffee, taken black, of course.

How delicious to find it also in cakes, truffles, chocolate bars, dragées, lollipops, *coussins*, like the famous ones from Lyon, created in 1897, an almond paste combined with curaçao-flavoured chocolate. Other chocolates are filled with praline, a mix of sugar, almonds, hazelnuts, vanilla, cocoa and milk chocolate. Or with *gianduja*, a creamy filling made of chocolate, hazelnuts, confectioner's (icing) sugar, and cocoa butter, which was invented in the Piedmont region of Italy in the 18th century. Finally, the picture wouldn't be complete without *ganache*, this soft blend of cream and chocolate, whose name comes from a famous anecdote. "Ganache!" was the insult hurled at an apprentice who had accidentally poured boiling cream over chocolate.

*"I want a chocolate cake,
black inside
from the chocolate."*

DONATIEN ALPHONSE, MARQUIS DE SADE (1740–1814)

At *Les Marquis*, the pairing of cocoa with other flavours reveals a palate of sweet subtleties: the cameos, chocolate medallions filled with rum-, chestnut honey-, rose-, violet-, or coconut-flavoured ganache. More minimalist, but no less sophisticated, *pavés* are sprinkled with sesame seeds, decorated with lemon confit, and flavoured with black tea. For their part, *boules* come in pistachio, verbena, maracuja pulp, and fleur de sel varieties. On the richer side, truffles conceal flavours of raspberry pulp, banyuls and spices, or grated coconut. Equally exotic, macarons are made of Jivara milk chocolate, white chocolate blended with passion fruit, or yuzu, a Japanese citrus whose flavour lies somewhere between lime, grapefruit and mandarin orange. A pairing with delicate Japanese whisky may even be in the works at Ladurée.

FACING PAGE
*Detail of boxes
and silk ribbons at*
Les Marquis de
Ladurée.

NEXT TWO PAGES
*Collection of Grand
Cru Chocolate
Macarons, made
with single-origin
chocolate from
Venezuela, Brazil,
Santo Domingo,
Colombia,
Madagascar, and
Ghana.*

Les Marquis de Ladurée
Les Marquis de Ladurée
Les Marquis de Ladurée

ome...

...olate treats to make at home...   Bonbons and

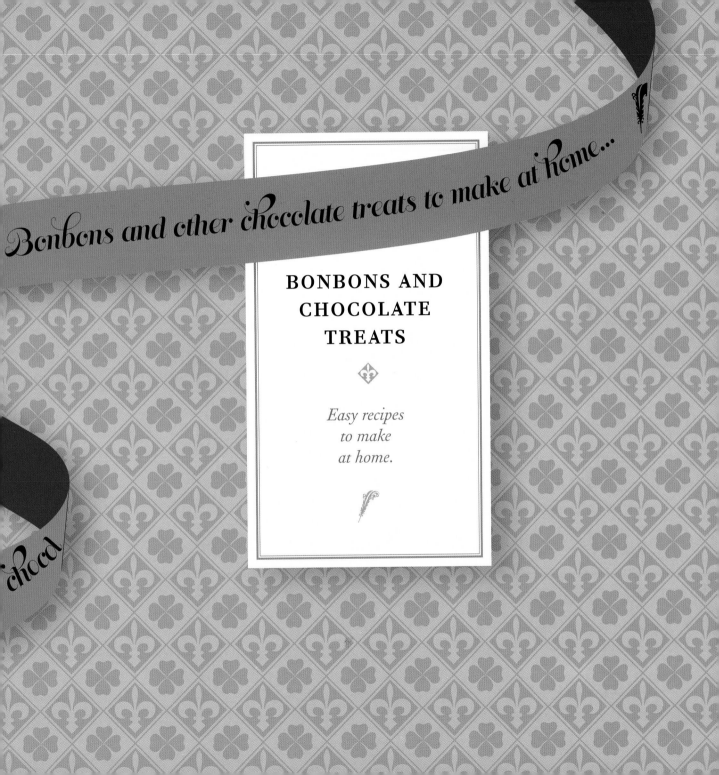

Bonbons and other chocolate treats to make at home...

BONBONS AND CHOCOLATE TREATS

❖

*Easy recipes
to make
at home.*

Dark Chocolate
TRUFFLES

MAKES 196 TRUFFLES

PREPARATION TIME: 2 HRS (OVER THE COURSE OF 3 DAYS) – COOKING TIME: 15 MIN

RESTING TIME: 24 HRS + 12 TO 24 HRS + 3 HRS

DARK CHOCOLATE GANACHE

750 g/1½ lb dark chocolate (56% cocoa)

450 g/16 oz heavy (double) cream

190 g/6¾ oz unsalted butter

100 g/3½ oz honey

COATING

About 500 g/17½ oz dark chocolate

About 200 g/7 oz cocoa powder

EQUIPMENT

34-cm/13½-inch square mould or
   baking sheet with a 1-cm/⅓-inch rim

Parchment paper

Chocolate thermometer

Ruler or 2-cm/¾-inch cookie cutter

DARK CHOCOLATE GANACHE

1   Chop the dark chocolate on a cutting board and transfer to a bowl. Cut the butter into small cubes and set aside. Heat up the cream with the honey. Delicately pour this warm mixture, a third at a time, over the chopped chocolate, stirring gently with a spatula. When the ganache is completely homogenous and has reached 35-40°C/95-105°F, incorporate the cubes of butter.

2   If you are using a mould, place it on top of a sheet of parchment paper. Otherwise, line a baking sheet with parchment paper or plastic wrap.

3   Pour the finished ganache into the mould, or onto the baking sheet. It is important to obtain a uniform 1-cm/⅓-inch-thick layer of ganache. Allow to set at a temperature of 12-15°C/54-59°F (in a cool cellar, for example), for 12 hours or overnight.

4   The next day, remove the mould (or un-mould the ganache from the baking sheet) and remove the parchment paper. Using a ruler or a square cookie cutter, cut out 2-cm/¾-inch squares of ganache. One by one, fold the squares in from the sides and shape them into truffles between the palms of your hands. Place them onto a

• • •

baking sheet lined with parchment paper, then allow to set again at 12-15°C/54-59°F for 12 to 24 hours.

Coating

1   Prepare a bowl of dark chocolate that has been tempered to 30°C/86°F (see technique p. 278). Pour the cocoa powder onto a plate.

2   Using a fork, dip the truffles, one by one, into the dark chocolate, then roll them in the cocoa powder until they are completely coated. Cool for at least 3 hours to set.

✤ Chef's Tips ✤

It is important to respect the different temperatures indicated in order to create a soft, creamy texture and to prolong the shelf life of the truffles.
To prevent the chocolate from burning, make sure to pour the honey-cream mixture over the chopped chocolate little by little, a half or a third at a time.
Store the truffles in an airtight container, in a dry place, between 12 and 15°C (54-59°F).
To fully appreciate these truffles, enjoy them at a temperature of about 20-22°C (68-72°F).

Coconut-Flavoured TRUFFLES

MAKES 196 TRUFFLES
PREPARATION TIME: 2 HRS (OVER THE COURSE OF 3 DAYS) – COOKING TIME: 15 MIN
RESTING TIME: 12 HRS + 12 TO 24 HRS + 3 HRS

COCONUT-FLAVOURED GANACHE

500 g/17½ oz white chocolate
62 g/2 oz heavy (double) cream
250 g/½ lb puréed coconut
100 g/3½ oz grated coconut
1 vanilla bean

COATING

about 600 g/21 oz white chocolate
about 200 g/7 oz powdered coconut

EQUIPMENT

34-cm/13½-inch square mould or baking
  sheet with an 8-mm rim
Parchment paper
Chocolate thermometer
Ruler or 2-cm/¾-inch square cookie
  cutter

COCONUT-FLAVOURED GANACHE

1 In a small saucepan, stir the puréed coconut into the cream. Split the vanilla bean and scrape the seeds into the coconut-cream mixture. Add the scraped bean. Warm over low heat. Remove the vanilla bean, then delicately pour the warmed mixture over the grated coconut. Allow to rest for 10 minutes.

2 While the coconut is soaking in the cream, melt the white chocolate in a bain-marie, or in the microwave, to a temperature of 40°C/105°F. Add the melted chocolate into the coconut-cream mixture, combining with a whisk.

3 If you are using a mould, place it on top of a sheet of parchment paper. Otherwise, line a baking sheet with parchment paper or plastic wrap.

4 When the ganache reaches 35°C/95°F and has gained a homogenous consistency, pour it into the mould, or onto the baking sheet. It is important to obtain a uniform 8-mm-thick layer of ganache. Allow to set at a temperature of 12-15°C/54-59°F (in a cool cellar, for example), for 12 hours or overnight.

• • •

5 The next day, remove the mould (or un-mould the ganache from
the baking sheet) and remove the parchment paper. Using a ruler or
a square cookie cutter, cut out 2-cm/¾-inch squares of ganache.
One by one, fold the squares in from the sides and shape them into
truffles between the palms of your hands. Place them on a baking
sheet lined with parchment paper, then allow to set again
at 12-15°C/54-59°F for 12 to 24 hours.

COATING
1 Prepare a bowl of white chocolate that has been tempered to
27°C/80°F (see technique p. 276). Pour the powdered coconut onto
a plate.

2 Using a fork, dip the truffles, one by one, into the white chocolate,
then roll them in the powdered coconut until they are completely
coated. Cool for at least 3 hours to set

❖ CHEF'S TIPS ❖

*It is important to respect the different temperatures indicated in order to create
a soft, creamy texture and to prolong the shelf life of the truffles. To prevent the
chocolate from burning, make sure to pour the coconut-cream mixture over the
melted white chocolate little by little, a half or a third at a time.*
*Store the truffles in an airtight container, in a dry place, between 12 and
15°C (54-59°F).*
*To fully appreciate these truffles, enjoy them at a temperature of about
20-22°C (68-72°F).*

Dark Chocolate
MENDIANTS
with nuts and candied fruit

MAKES 10 MENDIANTS
PREPARATION TIME: 40 MIN – COOKING TIME: 15 MIN – RESTING TIME: 3 HRS

350 g/¾ lb dark chocolate

40 whole, fresh pistachios

30 whole, raw hazelnuts

20 whole, raw almonds

10 walnut halves

40 golden raisins

40 small cubes of *orangettes*
(chocolate-dipped candied
orange peel)

EQUIPMENT
10 7-cm/2¾-inch tart moulds

Chocolate thermometer

Piping bag fitted with a
4-mm/⅛-inch tip

1 Start by roasting the almonds and hazelnuts separately. Preheat the oven to 180°C/360°F and scatter the almonds and hazelnuts onto two different baking sheets. Roast for 15 min. Once the nuts have taken on a nice golden colour, remove them from the oven and allow to cool to room temperature. Break the walnut halves in two, lengthwise.

2 Prepare a bowl of dark chocolate tempered to 30°C/86°F (see technique p. 276). Slide the melted chocolate into the piping bag.

3 Place one of the tart moulds on a scale. Pipe 30 g/1 oz of melted chocolate into the mould, then spread it out flat. Arrange a variety of nuts and fruit on the chocolate. Repeat with the other moulds. Allow to set at a temperature of 12-15°C/54-59°F (in a cool cellar, for example), for at least 3 hours.

❖ CHEF'S TIPS ❖
Take care to place the fruit and nuts onto the chocolate before it sets, to make sure they are firmly embedded. Store the mendiants in an airtight container, in a dry place, between 12 and 15°C (54-59°F). Enjoy them at a temperature of around 20°C/68°F to experience their full range of flavours.

Pistachio

Milk Chocolate Ganache BONBONS

MAKES 196 BONBONS
PREPARATION TIME: 1 HR (OVER THE COURSE OF 3 DAYS) – COOKING TIME: 15 MIN
RESTING TIME: 24 HRS + 12 HRS + 4 HRS

MILK CHOCOLATE GANACHE

915 g/2 lb milk chocolate
425 g/15 oz heavy (double) cream
140 g/5 oz unsalted butter
50 g/1¾ oz honey
100 g/3½ oz dark chocolate

COATING

About 500 g/17½ oz milk chocolate
About 50 g/1¾ oz cocoa powder

EQUIPMENT

34-cm/13½-inch square mould or baking
  sheet with a 1-cm/⅓-inch rim
Parchment paper
Chocolate thermometer
Ruler or 2-cm/¾-inch square cookie
  cutter

MILK CHOCOLATE GANACHE

1   Chop up the milk chocolate on a cutting board and transfer to a bowl. Cut the butter into small cubes and set aside. Heat the cream with the honey. Delicately pour this warm mixture, a third at a time, over the chopped chocolate, stirring gently with a spatula. When the ganache is completely homogenous and has reached 35-40°C/95-105°F, incorporate the cubes of butter.

2   If you are using a mould, place it on top of a sheet of parchment paper. Otherwise, line a baking sheet with parchment paper or plastic wrap.

3   Pour the finished ganache into the mould, or onto the baking sheet. It is important to obtain a uniform 1 cm/½-inch-thick layer of ganache. Allow to set at a temperature of 12-15°C/54-59°F (in a cool cellar, for example), for 24 hours.

4   The next day, remove the mould (or un-mould the ganache from the baking sheet) and remove the parchment paper. Prepare a bowl of dark chocolate tempered to 30°C/86°F (see technique p. 276). Use a spatula to spread a thin layer of chocolate onto both sides of the ganache. Then, using a ruler or a square cookie cutter, cut out 2-cm/¾-inch squares of ganache. Allow to dry at 12-15°C/54-59°F for 12 hours.

...

COATING

1 The third day, prepare a bowl of milk chocolate tempered to
   28°C/82°F (see technique p. 276).

2 Use a fork to dip the squares one by one into the milk chocolate,
   coating all sides. Place them onto a sheet of parchment paper or a
   silicone mat. Before the chocolate sets, use a sieve to coat them evenly
   with a fine layer of cocoa powder. Allow to harden for at least 4 hours.

❖ CHEF'S TIPS ❖

*It is important to respect the different temperatures indicated in order to create
a soft, creamy texture and to prolong the shelf life of the bonbons.*

*To prevent the chocolate from burning, make sure to pour the honey-cream
mixture over the chopped chocolate little by little, a half or a third at a time.*

*Store the bonbons in an airtight container, in a dry place, between 12 and
15°C (54-59°F).*

*To fully appreciate these bonbons, enjoy them at a temperature of about
20-22°C (68-72°F).*

Orange-flavoured chocolate-almond BONBONS

MAKES 196 BONBONS

PREPARATION TIME: 1 HR (OVER THE COURSE OF 3 DAYS) – COOKING TIME: 15 MIN

RESTING TIME: 24 HRS + 12 HRS + 4 HRS

ORANGE-FLAVOURED ALMOND PASTE

900 g/2 lb homemade almond paste
   (see recipe below)

900 g/2 lb candied orange peel
   (in thin slices or matchsticks)

4 g/1 tsp Grand Marnier (optional)

COATING AND DECORATION

About 600 g/21 oz dark chocolate

40 g/1½ oz raw almond slivers

150 g/5¼ oz candied orange peel
   (in matchsticks)

EQUIPMENT

Food processor

Stand mixer

34-cm/13½-inch square mould or baking
   sheet with a 1-cm/⅓-inch rim or two
   rules of the same height

• • •

ORANGE-FLAVOURED ALMOND PASTE

1 Transfer the candied orange peel to a food processor and mix until a paste forms. Combine this paste with the almond paste in the bowl of stand mixer equipped with a flat paddle, or combine well by hand. Flavour the mixture with Grand Marnier, if desired.

2 Use a rolling pin to spread the orange-flavoured almond paste out inside the rectangular frame, or between two rulers. It is important to obtain an even layer of paste, about 1-cm/½-in thick. To prevent the paste from sticking to the rolling pin, insert a sheet of parchment paper between the pin and the paste. Allow to dry at 12-15°C/54-59°F (in a cool cellar, for example) for 12 to 24 hours.

3 The next day, use the cookie cutter to cut the orange-flavoured almond paste into rounds. To prevent the paste from sticking to the cookie cutter, dip the cookie cutter in some Grand Marnier before using. Place the rounds one by one onto a sheet of parchment paper and allow to dry at 12-15°C/54-59°F for 12 hours.

• • •

Rolling pin

Parchment paper

Chocolate thermometer

3-cm/about 1 ¼-in round cookie cutter

COATING AND DECORATION

1   Start by roasting the almond slivers. Preheat oven to 180°C/360°F. Scatter the almond slivers out on a baking sheet and roast for 15 min. Once the nuts have taken on a nice golden colour, remove from oven and allow to cool to room temperature.

2   Slice the candied orange peel into 1 mm x 1 cm slivers (you will need 392 slivers). Set aside to dry before decorating.

3   Prepare a bowl of dark chocolate tempered to 30°C/86°F (see technique p. 276).

4   Use a three-tonged fork to dip the almond rounds one by one into the dark chocolate, then place them on a sheet of parchment paper. Before the chocolate hardens, decorate each round with 2 slivers of candied orange peel and 1 sliver of roasted almond. Allow to set for at least 4 hours.

❖ CHEF'S TIPS ❖

Store the bonbons in an airtight container, in a dry place, between 12 and 15 °C (54-59 °F). Enjoy them at a temperature of around 20-22 °C (68-72 °F), to experience their full range of flavours.

ALMOND PASTE

MAKES 900 G/2 lb ALMOND PASTE
PREPARATION TIME: 30 MIN – COOKING TIME: 15 MIN

1 Combine sugar, 135 g/4¾ oz of water, honey and glucose in a saucepan. Cook until the temperature of the mixture reaches 114°C/237°F.

2 Blitz the almonds in a food processor until they are reduced to a powder. When the sugar mixture reaches temperature, pour it over the powdered almonds and pulse to combine well.

3 When it starts to form a paste, turn it out onto a work surface and continue to knead it with your hands to obtain a homogenous mixture. Store the almond paste in an airtight container at 4°C/39°F.

565 g/1¼ lb whole, blanched almonds
270 g/9½ oz granulated sugar
60 g/2 oz honey
30 g/1 oz glucose syrup

EQUIPMENT
Sugar thermometer
Food processor

❖ CHEF'S TIPS ❖
Be careful not to over-mix the almond paste in the food processor, or the paste will become oily.
To save time, use store-bought almond paste.

Orange

Dark Chocolate
MENDIANT BITES
with nuts and candied fruit

MAKES ABOUT 50 PIECES
PREPARATION TIME: 40 MIN – COOKING TIME: 15 MIN – RESTING TIME: 3 HRS

1 Start by roasting the almonds and hazelnuts separately. Preheat the oven to 180°C/360°F and scatter the almonds and hazelnuts onto two different baking sheets. Roast for 15 min. Once the nuts have taken on a nice golden colour, remove them from the oven and allow to cool to room temperature.

2 Line a baking sheet with parchment paper or use a silicone mat. Prepare a bowl of dark chocolate tempered to 30°C/86°F (see technique p. 276). Slide the melted chocolate into the piping bag.

3 Pipe the melted chocolate out onto the sheet or mat in 2- to 2½-cm/ ¾- to 1-inch discs, until you run out of chocolate. Decorate each disc with a variety of nuts and fruit. Allow to set at a temperature of 12-15°C/54-59°F (in a cool cellar, for example), for at least 3 hours.

◈ CHEF'S TIPS ◈
Take care to place the fruit and nuts in the chocolate before it sets, to make sure they are firmly embedded. Store the mendiants in an airtight container, in a dry place, between 12 and 15 °C (54-59 °F). Enjoy them at a temperature of around 20 °C/68 °F, to experience their full range of flavours.

350 g/¾ lb dark chocolate
50 whole, fresh pistachios
50 whole, raw hazelnuts
50 whole, raw almonds
50 golden raisins
50 small cubes of *orangettes* (chocolate-dipped candied orange peel)

EQUIPMENT
Parchment paper or silicone mat
Chocolate thermometer
Piping bag fitted with a 4-mm/ ⅛-inch tip

VARIATIONS
You can also make these mendiants with milk chocolate or white chocolate, and use other fruits, like candied lemon, ginger, cashews, macadamia nuts...

Dark Chocolate
ROSES DES SABLES
with candied lemon peel

MAKES 45 PIECES

PREPARATION TIME: 40 MIN – COOKING TIME: 25 MIN – RESTING TIME: 3 HRS

250 g/½ lb milk chocolate

25 g/⅞ oz cocoa butter

250 g/½ lb raw almond slivers

110 g/4 oz candied lemon peel
  (in matchsticks)

40 g/1½ oz sugar

EQUIPMENT

Parchment paper

Chocolate thermometer

1   Start by making a syrup: Combine 35 g/1¼ oz of water with the sugar in a saucepan. Bring to a boil, stirring well to prevent the sugar from caramelizing on the bottom of the pan. Set aside to cool.

2   Glaze the almonds: Preheat the oven to 150°C/302°F. Stir the almonds into the cooled syrup, then spread them out in a single layer on a baking sheet lined with parchment paper. Roast for 15 minutes. Once they have taken on a nice golden colour, remove from oven and allow to cool to room temperature.

3   Meanwhile, cut the candied lemon peel matchsticks into 5-mm/⅕-inch cubes.

4   Prepare a bowl of dark chocolate tempered to 30°C/86°F (see technique p. 276). Melt the cocoa butter, then add to the tempered chocolate. In a separate bowl, use a spatula to mix the glazed almonds with the candied lemon peel cubes, then add the mixture of melted cocoa-butter and chocolate.

...

5 Line a baking sheet with parchment paper. Use two spoons to form little domes out of the mixture and place them on the parchment paper. Allow to set at a temperature of 12-15°C/54-59°F (in a cool cellar, for example), for at least 3 hours.

❖ Chef's Tips ❖

To prevent the chocolate from setting too quickly, temper the mixture of glazed almonds and candied lemon in the microwave for a few seconds before incorporating with the chocolate. Note: They shouldn't be warmer than the tempered chocolate, so as not to destabilize it.

Store the roses des sables in an airtight container, in a dry place, between 12 and 15°C (54-59°F). To fully appreciate these "desert roses," enjoy them at a temperature of about 20°C/68°F.

Milk Chocolate
ROSES DES SABLES
with candied lemon peel

MAKES 45 PIECES
PREPARATION TIME: 40 MIN – COOKING TIME: 25 MIN – RESTING TIME: 3 HRS

250 g/½ lb milk chocolate

25 g/⅞ oz cocoa butter

250 g/½ lb raw almond slivers

110 g/4 oz candied lemon peel
   (in matchsticks)

40 g/1½ oz sugar

EQUIPMENT

Parchment paper

Chocolate thermometer

1   Start by making a syrup: Combine 35 g/1¼ oz of water with the sugar in a saucepan. Bring to a boil, stirring well to prevent the sugar from caramelizing on the bottom of the pan. Set aside to cool.

2   Glaze the almonds: Preheat the oven to 150°C/302°F. Stir the almonds into the cooled syrup, then spread them out in a single layer on a baking sheet lined with parchment paper. Roast for 15 minutes. Once they have taken on a nice golden colour, remove from oven and allow to cool to room temperature.

3   Meanwhile, cut the candied lemon peel matchsticks into 5-mm/⅕-inch cubes.

4   Prepare a bowl of milk chocolate tempered to 30°C/86°F (see technique p. 276). Melt the cocoa butter, then add to the tempered chocolate. In a separate bowl, use a spatula to mix the glazed almonds with the candied lemon peel cubes, then add the mixture of melted cocoa-butter and chocolate.

...

5   Line a baking sheet with parchment paper. Use two spoons to form the mixture into little domes and place them on the parchment paper. Allow to set at a temperature of 12-15°C/54-59°F (in a cool cellar, for example), for at least 3 hours.

✦ Chef's Tips ✦

To prevent the chocolate from hardening too quickly, temper the mixture of glazed almonds and candied lemon in the microwave for a few seconds before incorporating with the chocolate. Note: They shouldn't be warmer than the tempered chocolate, so as not to destabilize it.

Store the roses des sables in an airtight container, in a dry place, between 12 and 15°C (54-59°F). To fully appreciate these "desert roses," enjoy them at a temperature of about 20°C/68°F.

Dark Chocolate
TUILES

MAKES 60 TUILES

PREPARATION TIME: 30 MIN – COOKING TIME: 30 MIN – RESTING TIME: 3 HRS

500 g/17½ oz dark chocolate
135 g/4¾ oz chopped raw almonds
125 g/4½ oz sugar

EQUIPMENT
Piping bag fitted with a 20-mm/
   ¾-inch tip
Parchment paper
Sugar thermometer
Chocolate thermometer

1 Start by roasting the chopped almonds. Preheat the oven to 180°C/360°F and spread the chopped almonds out in a single layer on a baking sheet. Roast for 15 min. Once the nuts have taken on a nice golden colour, remove from oven and allow to cool to room temperature.

2 Caramelize the almonds: Combine 25 g/⅞ oz of water and the sugar in a saucepan and cook to 114°C/237°F on the sugar thermometer. Once the mixture reaches temperature, remove from heat and incorporate the chopped almonds. Use a spatula to combine until the almonds are completely coated with sugar. Return to heat and caramelize, stirring well to prevent burning. When the almonds start to take on a nice colour, remove from heat and continue to stir to separate the almond pieces. Allow to cool.

3 Use scissors or a knife to cut out 7-cm/2¾-inch x 30-cm/11¾-inch strips of parchment paper.

4 Prepare a bowl of dark chocolate tempered to 30°C/86°F (see technique p. 276) and add 75 g/2½ oz of caramelized chopped almonds.

...

5   Use a dough scraper to help slide the mixture into the piping bag. On one strip of parchment paper, pipe out 4 evenly-spaced discs of batter. Take hold of one end of the strip in each hand and tap the strip gently on the work surface to obtain uniform, flat discs. Before the chocolate hardens, lay the strip of *tuiles* on top of a rolling pin (or any other cylinder with a 40-mm/1¾-inch diameter), such that it takes on the rounded shape of the pin. Once the chocolate has hardened, remove from the rolling pin and allow to set at 12-15°C/54-59°F (in a cool cellar, for example), for at least 3 hours.

❖ Chef's Tips ❖

To prevent the chocolate from hardening too quickly, temper the caramelized almonds in the microwave for a few seconds before incorporating with the chocolate. Note: They shouldn't be warmer than the tempered chocolate, so as not to destabilize it.

Store the tuiles in an airtight container, in a dry place, between 12 and 15°C (54-59°F). To fully appreciate their flavour, enjoy them at a temperature of about 20°C/68°F.

Chocolate-Coated BÂTONS DE MARÉCHAL *Cookies*

BISCUIT DOUGH

90 g/3 oz confectioner's (icing) sugar
30 g/1 oz granulated sugar
12 g/½ oz fine pastry flour (T45)
90 g/3 oz powdered almonds
200 g/7 oz chopped almonds
3 egg whites

CHOCOLATE

400 g dark chocolate (70% cocoa)

EQUIPMENT

Food processor
Electric whisk
Parchment paper
Piping bag fitted with a 10-mm tip
Stainless steel angled spatula
Chocolate thermometer

COOKIE BATTER

1 Start by combining the almond powder with the confectioner's (icing) sugar in the food processor. Mix to obtain a very fine powder. Then combine this powder with the flour, passing the mixture through a sieve.

2 Beat the egg whites into a thick foam, then add one-third of the granulated sugar (10 g/⅓ oz) and continue to beat until the sugar is dissolved. Add another third of the sugar, beat for another minute, then add the rest of the sugar and beat again for another minute.

3 Using a soft spatula, gently incorporate the almond powder-sugar-flour mixture into the egg whites.

4 Preheat the oven to 160°C/320°F. Line a baking sheet with parchment paper. Fill the piping bag with the biscuit batter and pipe out 7-cm/2¾-inch long strips onto the parchment paper. Scatter chopped almonds over each strip. Bake for 18-20 minutes. When the cookies are done, remove from oven and allow to cool on a baking rack.

...

Chocolate

1   The process of achieving the perfect "tempered-melted" chocolate is always quite delicate. Here is a simple method: use a big knife to chop the chocolate on a cutting board, then melt it over a bain-marie, while stirring continuously with a spatula.

2   Pour ¾ of the melted chocolate out onto a clean, dry work surface. Using a stainless-steel angled spatula, spread the chocolate out and scrape it back up, working it back and forth, until the chocolate starts to thicken.

3   Return the chocolate to the bowl with the remaining ¼ and combine to homogenize well, until the temperature of the chocolate reaches 30-31°C/86-88°F. If it is too hot or too cold, it will turn white as it cools.

4   Dip the cookies into the chocolate, then set them on a baking rack to harden. Store in an airtight container.

Facing page

The Marquis and Marquise de Montsoreau.

Watercolour, Louis Carrogis, known as Carmontelle, 1780.

Dark Chocolate-Coated
CANDIED GINGER CHIPS

MAKES 50 PIECES
PREPARATION TIME: 45 MIN – RESTING TIME: 3 HRS

500 g/17½ oz dark chocolate
3 pieces of whole candied ginger

EQUIPMENT
Mandolin
Kitchen tweezers
Parchment paper or silicone mat
Chocolate thermometer

1 Hold the pieces of candied ginger lengthwise and use a mandolin (or chef's knife) to cut them into 1-mm thin slices. You should almost be able to see through each slice.

2 Prepare a bowl of dark chocolate tempered to 30°C/86°F (see technique p. 276).

3 Using a pair of kitchen tweezers, dip the ginger slices one by one into the chocolate, letting the excess drip off, then place them on a sheet of parchment paper or a silicone mat. Repeat until you have used all of the ginger "chips". Allow to set at a temperature of 12-15°C/54-59°F (in a cool cellar, for example), for at least 3 hours.

❖ CHEF'S TIPS ❖
Store the chocolate ginger chips in an airtight container, in a dry place, between 12 and 15°C (54-59°F). Enjoy them at a temperature of around 20°C/68°F, to experience their full range of flavours.

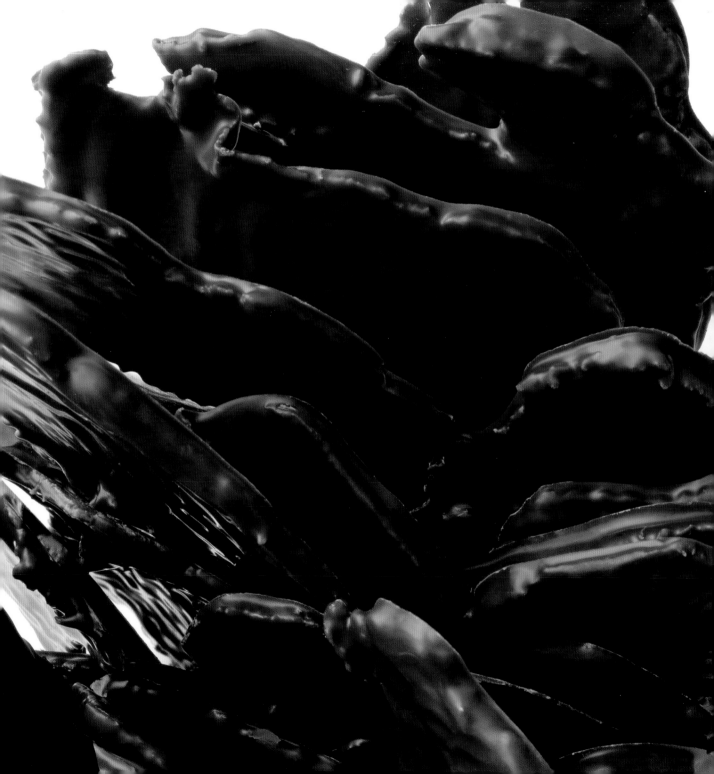

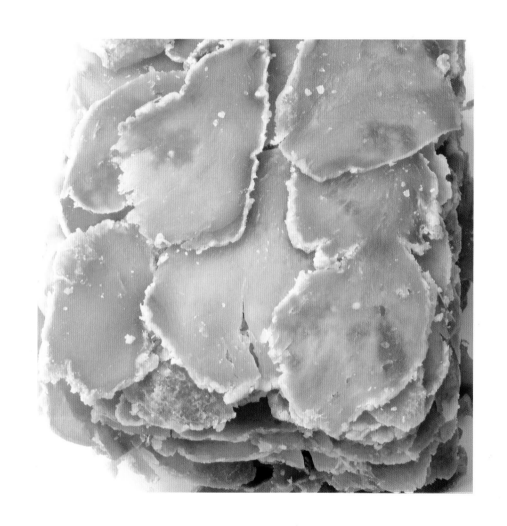

Ginger

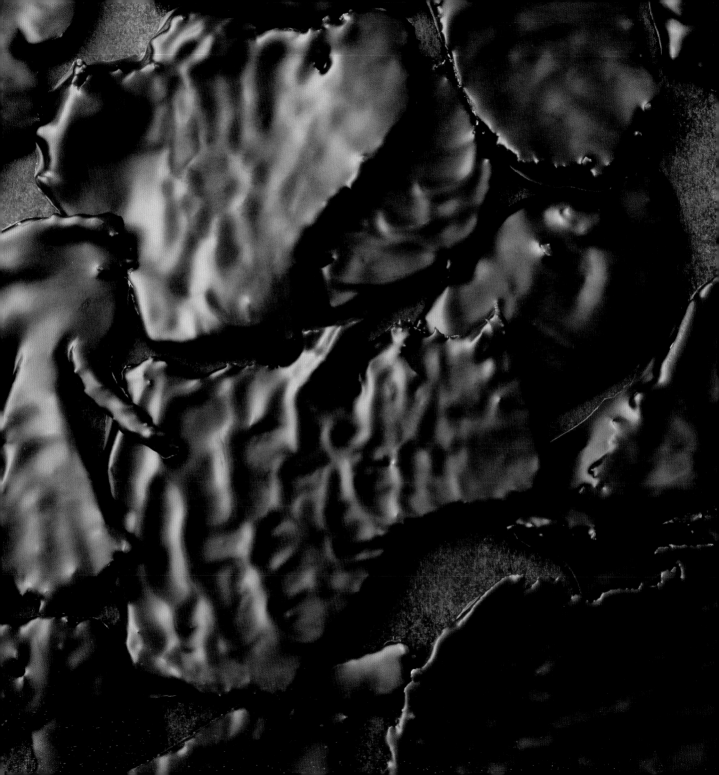

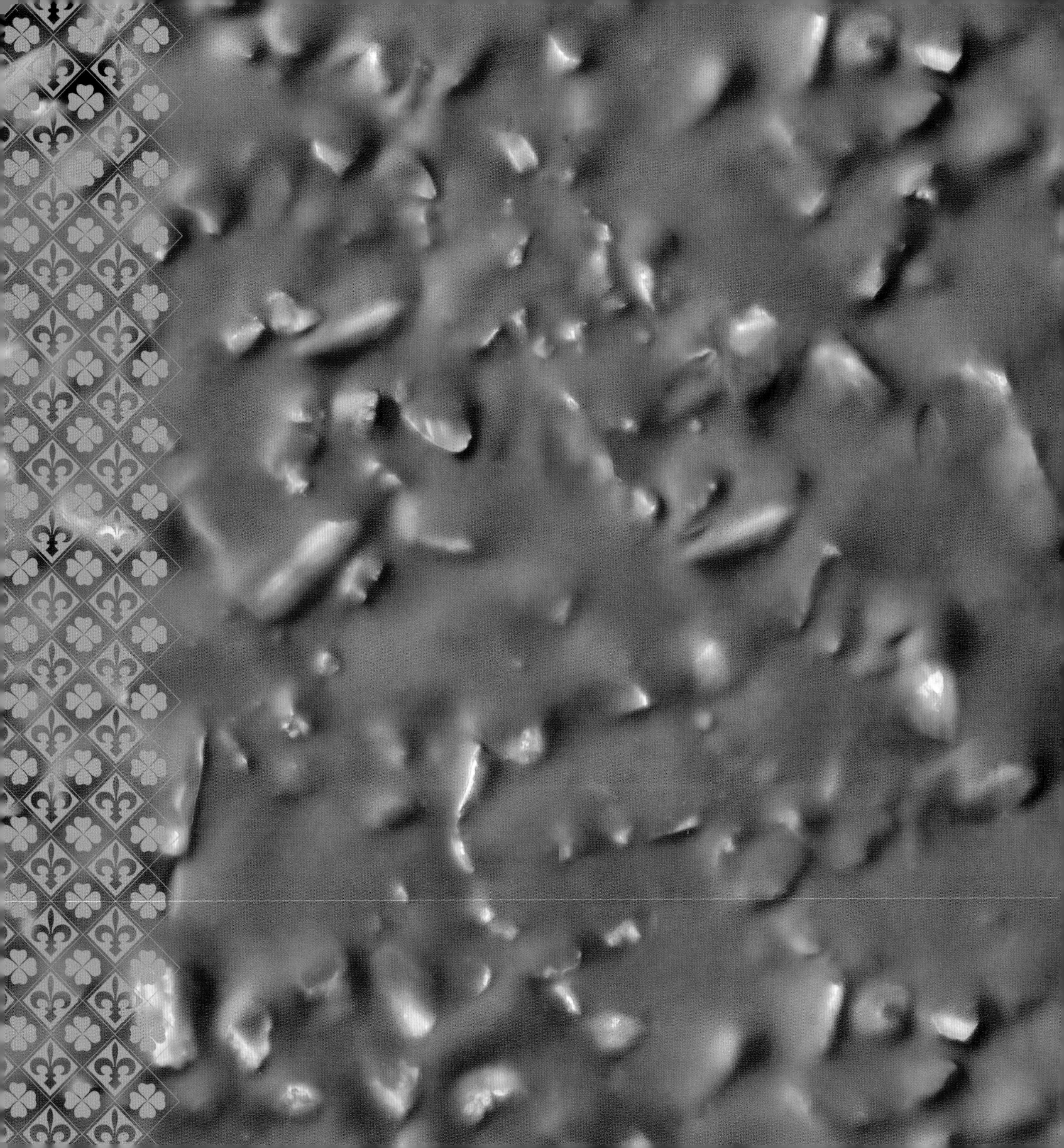

Milk Chocolate BAR *with Almonds*

MAKES 1 SHEET
PREPARATION TIME: 30 MIN – COOKING TIME: 15 MIN – RESTING TIME: 3 HRS

1 Roast the almonds: Preheat the oven to 180°C/360°F and spread the raw almond slivers out in a single layer on a baking sheet. Roast for 15 min. Once the nuts have taken on a nice golden colour, remove from oven and allow to cool to room temperature.

2 If you are using a mould, place it on top of a sheet of parchment paper. Otherwise, line a baking sheet with parchment paper or plastic wrap.

3 Prepare a bowl of milk chocolate tempered to 28°C/82°F (see technique p. 276). Stir in the roasted almonds. Pour the mixture out onto the baking sheet or into the mould, then tap the baking sheet or parchment paper gently on the work surface, or use a spatula or dough scraper to spread the chocolate-almond mixture evenly. The goal is to obtain an even layer, about 4 mm/⅛ inch thick.

4 Allow to set at a temperature of 12-15°C/54-59°F (in a cool cellar, for example), for at least 3 hours. Un-mould the chocolate or remove the baking mould.

800 g/1¼ lb milk chocolate
200 g/7 oz almond slivers, preferably raw

EQUIPMENT
34-cm/13½-inch square mould or baking sheet with a 4-mm/⅛-inch rim
Parchment paper
Chocolate thermometer
Spatula or dough scraper

❖ CHEF'S TIPS ❖
To prevent the chocolate from hardening too quickly, temper the almonds in the microwave for a few seconds before incorporating with the chocolate. Note: They shouldn't be warmer than the tempered chocolate, so as not to destabilize it.

Almond

Dark Chocolate
BAR
with Hazelnuts

MAKES 1 SHEET

PREPARATION TIME: 30 MIN – COOKING TIME: 15 MIN – RESTING TIME: 3 HRS

800 g/1¼ lb dark chocolate
200 g/7 oz whole, raw almonds

EQUIPMENT

34-cm/13½-inch square mould or baking
   sheet with a 4-mm/⅛-inch rim
Food processor or rolling pin
Sieve
Parchment paper
Chocolate thermometer
Spatula or dough scraper

❖ CHEF'S TIPS ❖

*Store the bars in an airtight
container, in a dry place, between
12 and 15 °C (54-59 °F). Enjoy at a
temperature of around 20 °C/68 °F.*

1 Roast the hazelnuts: Preheat the oven to 180°C/360°F and spread the raw hazelnuts out in a single layer on a baking sheet. Roast for 15 min. Once the nuts have taken on a nice golden colour, remove from oven and allow to cool to room temperature.

2 Using a food processor or a rolling pin, roughly crush the hazelnuts, then pass them through a sieve to remove the powdered residue and keep only the hazelnut pieces.

3 If you are using a mould, place it on top of a sheet of parchment paper. Otherwise, line a baking sheet with parchment paper or plastic wrap.

4 Prepare a bowl of dark chocolate tempered to 30-31°C/86-88°F (see technique p. 276). Stir in the crushed roasted hazelnuts. Pour the mixture out onto the baking sheet or into the mould, then tap the baking sheet or parchment paper gently on the work surface, or use a spatula or dough scraper to spread the chocolate-hazelnut mixture evenly. The goal is to obtain an even layer, about 4 mm/⅛ inch thick.

5 Allow to set at a temperature of 12-15°C/54-59°F (in a cool cellar, for example), for at least 3 hours. Un-mould the chocolate or remove the baking mould.

Hazelnut

White Chocolate and Passion Fruit MACARONS

MAKES ABOUT 50 MACARONS
PREPARATION TIME: 2 HRS (OVER THE COURSE OF 2 DAYS) – COOKING TIME: 13 MIN
RESTING TIME: 12 HRS

MACARON COOKIES
275 g/10 oz powdered almond
250 g/9 oz confectioner's (icing) sugar
6 egg whites
210 g/7½ oz granulated sugar

WHITE CHOCOLATE AND PASSION FRUIT GANACHE
300 g/10½ oz white chocolate
65 g/2¼ oz heavy (double) cream
25 g/⅞ oz unsalted butter
65 g/2¼ oz passion fruit juice
10 g/⅓ oz honey

EQUIPMENT
Piping bag fitted with a 10-mm tip

MACARON COOKIES

1 Start by combining the powdered almond and confectioner's (icing) sugar in a food processor. Mix to obtain a very fine powder. Pass through a sieve.

2 Beat the egg whites into a thick foam, using an electric whisk. Add one-third of the granulated sugar (70 g/2½ oz) and continue to beat until the sugar is dissolved. Add another third of the sugar, beat for another minute, then add the rest of the sugar and beat again for another minute.

3 Using a soft spatula, gently fold the almond powder-sugar mixture into the egg whites. Combine such that the batter falls slightly, barely softening.

4 Transfer the batter to the piping bag and pipe 3- to 4-cm/ 1- to 1½-inch discs out onto the parchment paper. Tap the baking sheet lightly to finish spreading the macaron discs.

...

5   Preheat the oven to 150°C/302°F. Allow the macarons to rest at room temperature for 10 minutes, then bake them for 13 minutes, until they slightly begin to set.

6   Remove from oven, then use a glass to pour a little bit of water between the parchment paper and the baking sheet, lifting the paper up carefully at each corner. The humidity and steam created by the water on the hot sheet will make it easier to lift the macarons. Wait until they have completely cooled, then remove half of the cookies and place them upside down on a plate.

WHITE CHOCOLATE AND PASSION FRUIT GANACHE

1   On a cutting board, finely chop the white chocolate with a chef's knife, then transfer the chopped chocolate to a bowl and set aside. Combine the cream, honey, and passion fruit juice in a saucepan and bring to a boil. Pour this mixture, a third at a time, over the chopped chocolate, stirring well with a spatula between each third to make a thoroughly homogenous mixture.

⟡ CHEF's TIPS ⟡

It is strongly recommended to refrigerate the macarons overnight before serving. This allows for the osmosis of the different components, which develops and refines their taste and texture.

2   Cut the butter into small pieces and incorporate into the ganache to obtain a very smooth mixture. Transfer to a baking dish and cover by applying plastic wrap directly onto the surface of the ganache. Refrigerate for 1 hour, until it has the consistency of a smooth cream.

3   Transfer the ganache to a piping bag and pipe a hazelnut-sized amount onto each of the overturned macaron halves. Top with the remaining macarons.

Chocolate FINANCIERS

25 g/⅞ oz dark chocolate (70% cocoa)

80 g/3 oz unsalted butter + 20 g/¾ oz for the moulds

150 g/5¼ oz confectioner's (icing) sugar

40 g/1½ oz flour (T55)

3 pinches of baking powder

50 g/1¾ oz powdered almonds

15 g/½ oz cocoa powder

4 egg whites

EQUIPMENT

9- by 4-cm/3½- by 1½-inch baking moulds

Piping bag fitted with a 12-mm/½-inch plain tip

1   Melt 80 g/3 oz of unsalted butter in a small saucepan. At the same time, melt the dark chocolate over a bain-marie in a separate bowl.

2   In another bowl, combine the confectioner's (icing) sugar, powdered almonds, baking powder, cocoa powder, and flour, then slowly add the egg whites, stirring constantly with a spatula to prevent lumps from forming. Add the warm melted butter and the melted chocolate and mix well. Refrigerate the resulting batter for at least 12 hours or overnight.

3   The next day, preheat the oven to 210°C/410°F. Melt the remaining 20 g/¾ oz of butter and use a brush to butter the moulds. Transfer the batter to the piping bag and fill each mould to about three-quarters.

4   Bake for 6 to 8 minutes. Remove the financiers from the oven and allow to cool slightly. Un-mould and place on a baking rack to cool completely.

Chocolate
MERINGUES

MAKES 20-22 MERINGUES
PREPARATION TIME: 20 MIN – COOKING TIME: 2 ½ HRS

150 g/5¼ oz granulated sugar
7 g/¼ oz corn starch (flour)
8 g/⅓ oz cocoa powder
4 egg whites
20 g/¾ oz cocoa nibs

EQUIPMENT
Electric whisk
Piping bag fitted with a 10-mm star tip

❖ CHEF'S TIPS ❖
*Lightly dust the meringues with
cocoa powder and serve
with a scoop of ice cream or sorbet.*

1 Preheat the oven to 100°C/212°F. Combine the corn starch (flour) with the cocoa powder, pass the powders through a sieve, then add 30 g/1 oz of granulated sugar to the mixture.

2 Beat the egg whites in a mixing bowl with an electric whisk. When they are nice and foamy, add 40 g/1½ oz granulated sugar and continue to beat into stiff peaks. Add another 40 g/1½ oz sugar and beat for 1 minute. Add the last 40 g/1½ oz of sugar and beat for 1 more minute. Use a spatula to fold the cocoa-powder mixture into the egg whites.

3 Transfer to the piping bag and pipe twists of meringue out onto a baking sheet lined with parchment paper. The meringues will puff up in the oven, so take care to leave adequate space between each one. If you don't have a piping bag , you can use 2 tablespoons dipped in hot water to form the meringues.

4 Scatter cocoa nibs over each meringue, then bake for about 2 ½ hours. The meringues should cook slowly and be completely dry. Remove from oven and allow to cool. Store in an airtight container.

Chocolate-Raspberry
VERRINES

RASPBERRY JAM

800 g fresh raspberries

280 g granulated sugar

SOFT CHOCOLATE COOKIE

75 g/2½ oz dark chocolate (70% cocoa)

80 g/3 oz unsalted butter

1 whole egg

2 egg yolks

3 egg whites

80 g/3 oz granulated sugar

25 g/⅞ oz fine pastry flour (T45)

1 Tbsp cocoa powder

CHOCOLATE MOUSSE

320 g/11 oz dark chocolate (70% cocoa)

80 g/3 oz unsalted butter

8 eggs

80 g/3 oz granulated sugar

A pinch of salt

RASPBERRY JAM

1   Wash the raspberries thoroughly and drain. Transfer to a saucepan with the sugar and cook for 4 minutes, then allow to cool completely.

SOFT CHOCOLATE COOKIE

1   Use a chef's knife to chop up the dark chocolate on a cutting board. Transfer to a bowl over a bain-marie. Melt the chocolate with the butter, without overheating the mixture, stirring with a spatula. Remove from the bain-marie. Pass the flour and the cocoa powder together through a sieve into another bowl.

2   Preheat the oven to 180°C/360°F. Combine the egg, the egg yolks, and 40 g/1½ oz of granulated sugar in a bowl over a bain-marie, whisking to combine until the mixture turns white.

3   Remove from the bain-marie and reserve. Quickly beat the egg whites to a thick white foam, add the remaining sugar and whisk for another minute.

4   Gently fold one-third of the egg-yolk-sugar mixture into the melted chocolate, then pour over the remaining two-thirds of the egg-yolk-sugar mixture, again combining gently. Then, gently fold in one-third

...   ...

CHOCOLATE CREAM

160 g/5½ oz dark chocolate (70% cocoa)
125 g/4½ oz milk
125 g/4½ oz cream (single)
3 egg yolks
25 g/⅞ oz granulated sugar

EQUIPMENT

Electric whisk
3 piping bags with 3 8-mm plain tips
Chocolate thermometer
Cooking thermometer
Cookie cutter

of the beaten egg whites, and the cocoa powder-flour mixture. Pour the resulting mixture over the remaining two-thirds of the beaten egg whites, folding everything together delicately.

5   Line a baking sheet with parchment paper, then spread the batter out to create an even 1-cm/⅓-inch thick layer. Bake for 12 minutes. Remove from oven and allow to cool.

6   Use a cookie cutter to cut out 12 cookies, less than 1 cm/⅓-inch in diameter (depending on the size of your verrines).

CHOCOLATE MOUSSE

1   Use a chef's knife to chop up the dark chocolate on a cutting board. Transfer to a bowl over a bain-marie. Cut the butter into small pieces and stir into the melting chocolate. When the chocolate and butter are completely melted and incorporated, remove from the bain-marie and allow to cool to lukewarm (18-20°C/64-68°F on a chocolate thermometer).

2   Break the eggs and separate the whites from the yolks. Reserve the whites. Lightly beat the yolks to liquefy.

3   Add a pinch of salt to the white, then beat them into a thick white foam. Add the sugar and continue to beat into stiff peaks.

4   Quickly, but gently, incorporate the yolks with a whisk (without whisking!), making sure to dip down into the centre of the bowl and around the sides to create a homogenous mixture.

5   Use a soft spatula to gently fold ¼ of this egg mixture into the melted chocolate. Pour over the remaining ¾ of the egg mixture, continuing to fold the mixture gently, dipping down into the centre and around the sides to bring the mousse towards the centre.

CHOCOLATE CREAM

1   Whisk the sugar with the egg yolks until the mixture turns white.

2   Bring the milk and cream to a simmer in a saucepan. Pour part of this hot liquid over the creamed yolks, stirring vigorously. Return the mixture to the saucepan and cook over low heat. The temperature of the mixture should rise to about 84°C/183°F on a cooking thermometer. Meanwhile, use a chef's knife to chop the chocolate finely and transfer to a bowl.

3   Pour the hot "crème anglaise" from the saucepan over the chopped chocolate, mixing with a spatula. Use a hand blender to mix more thoroughly if necessary.

ASSEMBLY

1   Slide each preparation (jam, mousse, cream) into a separate piping bag fitted with an 8-mm tip.

2   Place the equivalent of 1 cm/⅓ inch of jam in the bottom of a verrine, then place it in the freezer for 10 minutes. This first layer must set before proceeding to the second, or the layers will blur, instead of creating neat stripes.

• • •

3   Add a bit of chocolate cream, then return the verrine to the freezer for
another 10 minutes. Finally, add a layer of chocolate mousse, and top
it off with a cookie, then a little bit more mousse (the cookie should
not be visible, sandwiched inside the mousse). Return to the freezer
for another 10 minutes.

4   Repeat these 3 steps one more time, then finish with a layer of
raspberry jam. Repeat for the other 5 verrines. Decorate as desired.

❖ Chef's Tips ❖
*To fully appreciate the verrines, remove them from the refrigerator
5 to 7 minutes before serving. They'll be perfect.*

Extra Dark Chocolate
SORBET

MAKES 1 LITRE OF SORBET
PREPARATION TIME: 20 MIN – RESTING TIME: 45 MIN

190 g/6¾ oz extra dark chocolate
   (85% cocoa)
150 g/5¼ oz granulated sugar
25 g/⅞ oz honey
15 g/½ oz cocoa nibs

EQUIPMENT
Food processor
Ice cream or sorbet maker
1 litre ice cream container

1   Use a chef's knife to chop the dark chocolate finely on a cutting board, then transfer to a bowl.

2   Bring 600 g/21 oz water, the granulated sugar and honey to a boil in a saucepan. Pour the mixture over the chopped chocolate, stirring lightly with a spatula. Cover with a sheet of plastic wrap placed directly on the surface of the mixture. Refrigerate for 45 minutes.

3   Once the mixture has cooled, transfer to an ice cream or sorbet maker. Once the sorbet has set, use a spatula to fold in the cocoa nibs, then transfer to the ice cream container. Store in the freezer at -18°C.

❖ CHEF'S TIPS ❖
If possible, enjoy and finish the sorbet the same day it was made to appreciate its incomparable texture.
If it must be stored in the freezer, remove it 10 minutes before serving to soften.

FACING PAGE

The Marquis d'Étampes.

WATERCOLOUR, LOUIS CARROGIS, KNOWN AS CARMONTELLE, 1764.

Dark Chocolate CRÈME BRÛLÉE

SERVES 4
PREPARATION AND COOKING TIME: 25 MIN – RESTING TIME: 12 HRS

110 g/4 oz dark chocolate (70% cocoa)
225 g/8 oz whole milk
250 g/½ lb liquid crème fraîche
3 egg yolks
50 g/1¾ oz granulated sugar
60 g/2 oz brown sugar

EQUIPMENT
4 oven-safe ramekins

1 Use a chef's knife to finely chop the chocolate. Reserve. In a bowl, beat the egg yolks with the sugar until the mixture turns very white.

2 Combine the milk and cream in a saucepan and bring to a simmer. Stir in the chopped chocolate, then pour over the egg yolk-sugar mixture and combine well.

3 Preheat the oven to 100°C/212°F. Pour an equal amount of the cream into each ramekin, then place the ramekins in an oven-proof baking dish. Pour enough water into the baking dish to reach 5 mm from the top of the ramekins. Bake in this bain-marie for 1 hour. Use a knife to check the cream. The cream is done when it is set, but still jiggling.

4 Remove from oven and allow to cool. Then cover the ramekins with plastic wrap to prevent the formation of humidity on the cream. Refrigerate for at least 12 hours.

5 Before serving, preheat the broiler. Cover the cream with a layer of brown sugar, then broil for 2 minutes to caramelize the sugar. When the sugar has turned a nice brown colour, remove from oven and serve immediately.

Chocolate
RICE PUDDING

SERVES 6

PREPARATION TIME: 50 MIN – COOKING TIME: 30 MIN – RESTING TIME: 1 HR OR MORE

180 ground Italian rice
1 litre whole milk
100 g/3½ oz granulated sugar
70 g/2½ oz dark chocolate
   (85% cocoa)
½ vanilla bean
A pinch of fine sea salt

1 Rinse the rice under cold water. Bring a pot of water to a boil and cook the rice for 1 minute. Drain.

2 Pour the milk into another pot. Add the salt. Split the ½ vanilla bean and scrape the seeds into the milk, then add the bean and bring the milk to a boil. Add the drained rice and the sugar. Cook over low heat for about 30 minutes, until the rice has absorbed a good portion of the liquid. Remove from heat.

3 Use a chef's knife to finely chop the chocolate, then add it to the rice. Stir with a spatula to obtain a homogenous mixture. Transfer the rice pudding into a big baking dish and cover with plastic wrap to prevent it from drying out and forming a crust. Allow to cool.

4 Refrigerate for at least 1 hour before serving. Fill the ramekins and serve cold.

❖ CHEF'S TIPS ❖
If you find that your pudding is too firm, you can soften it by adding one or two spoonfuls of whole milk.

Chocolate CREAM FILLING

MAKES 500 G/17½ OZ

PREPARATION TIME: 20 MIN – COOKING TIME: 5 MIN

100 g/3½ oz dark chocolate (85% cocoa)
250 g/½ lb whole milk + 15 g for the final step
50 g/1¾ oz heavy (double) cream
2 egg yolks
35 g/1¼ oz granulated sugar
15 g/½ oz corn starch (flour)

1   Use a chef's knife to finely chop the chocolate. Reserve.

2   Whisk the egg yolks with the sugar until the mixture begins to turn white. Add the corn starch (flour).

3   Combine the milk and cream in a saucepan and bring to a boil. Pour half of this hot liquid over the egg-sugar mixture and stir vigorously. Return this mixture to the saucepan and bring to a boil, stirring with a whisk and taking care to scrape along the sides of the pan.

4   Remove from heat and transfer to a bowl. Allow to cool for 10 minutes so that the cream remains hot, but not boiling, then stir in the chopped chocolate. Cover with plastic wrap and refrigerate.

5   Once the cream is cold, stir in 15 g/½ oz of whole milk with a spatula. The cream will be smooth and shiny and ready for use.

❖ CHEF'S TIPS ❖
You can use this cream to fill pastries like choux, millefeuilles, etc…

Chocolate Whipped Cream

Makes 970g/34 oz of Chantilly cream
Preparation time: 15 min – Resting time: 24 h

200 g/7 oz dark chocolate (70% cocoa)
120 g/4 oz whole milk
600 g/21 oz heavy (double) cream
50 g/1¾ oz granulated sugar

Equipment
Hand blender
Electric whisk

1 Use a chef's knife to finely chop the chocolate, then transfer it to a bowl.

2 Combine the milk, cream and sugar in a saucepan and bring to a boil. Pour the hot liquid, a third at a time, over the chopped chocolate, stirring with a wooden spatula between each third, to obtain a homogenous mixture. Mix briefly with a hand blender.

3 Cover with plastic wrap laid directly onto the surface of the cream. Refrigerate for 24 hours.

4 The next day, use an electric whisk to whip the cream. You will notice that the first few turns of the whisk will liquify the mixture. Don't be alarmed – this is normal. As you continue to whip the cream, it will begin to take on a lighter, thicker texture.

❖ Chef's Tips ❖
Use this whipped cream to decorate desserts, or serve alongside a scoop of vanilla ice cream, for example.

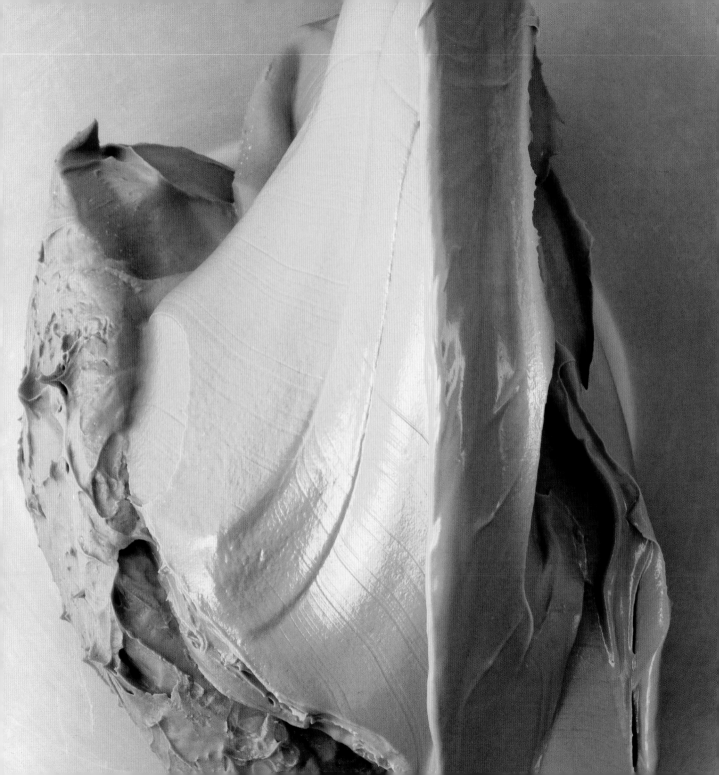

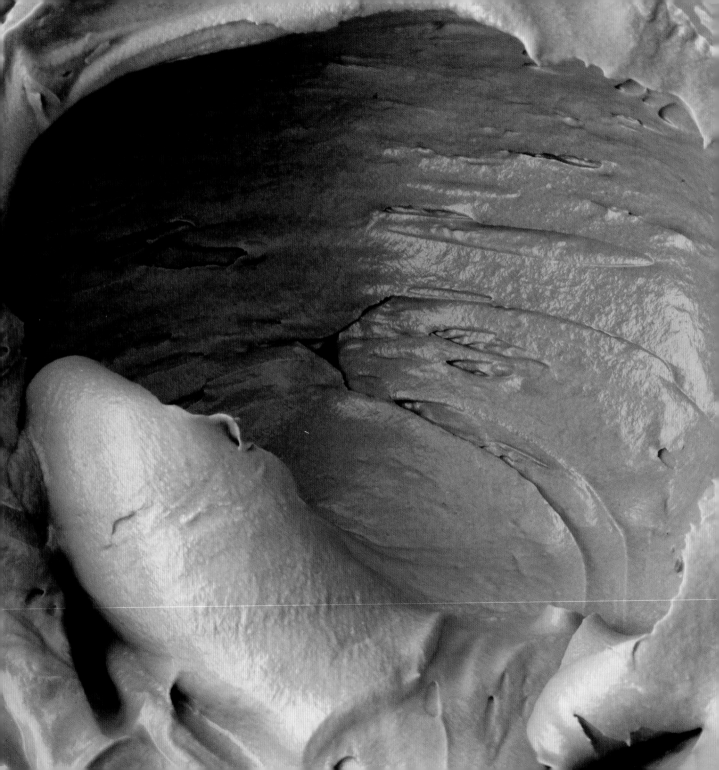

Classic
BROWNIE

SERVES 4
PREPARATION TIME: 15 MIN – COOKING TIME: 15 TO 16 MIN

1 Preheat the oven to 160°C/320°F. Use a chef's knife to finely chop the chocolate, then melt it over a bain-marie (or in the microwave). Cut the butter into small cubes and melt in the microwave.

2 Whisk the eggs and the sugar together in a bowl until they turn white, then add the melted chocolate and butter. Mix with a soft spatula. Sift in the flour through a sieve, combine well, then add the pecan pieces.

3 Transfer the batter to the mould and bake for about 15 minutes. Remove from oven and allow to cool.

80 g/3 oz bittersweet chocolate (67% cocoa)
110 g/4 oz unsalted butter
2 whole eggs
50 g/1¾ oz granulated sugar
55 g/2 oz all-purpose flour (T55)
100 g/3½ oz pecan pieces

EQUIPMENT
Deep baking mould

❖ CHEF'S TIPS ❖
To make the brownie easier to cut, put it in the freezer for a few minutes before serving. Enjoy with a nice vanilla-flavoured crème anglaise.

Chocolate CAKE

55 g/2 oz fine pastry flour (T45)

15 g/½ oz cocoa powder

4 g/1 tsp baking powder

60 g/2 oz heavy (double) cream

40 g/1½ oz melted butter

125 g/4½ oz whole eggs

35 g/1¼ oz honey

65 g/2¼ oz granulated sugar

37 g/1 ⅓ oz powdered almond

25 g/⅞ oz cocoa nibs (optional)

35 g/1¼ oz dark chocolate
   (70% cocoa), chopped

30 g/1 oz dark chocolate
   (70% cocoa), melted

EQUIPMENT

25 x 8 x 8 cm/10 x 3 x 3 inch cake mould

Parchment paper

Guitar sheets for working the chocolate

Angled spatula

Piping bag fitted with a 12-mm/½-inch
   tip

1   Butter the cake mould, then line with a rectangle of parchment paper to make it easier to remove the cake. Refrigerate the mould for 10 minutes to harden the butter. Remove from the refrigerator and flour the mould, turning it upside down to tap out the excess.

2   Pass the cocoa powder, flour, and baking powder through a sieve into a bowl and combine.

3   In another bowl, whisk the eggs, honey and sugar together, until the mixture turns very white. Stir in the powdered almond, the cocoa nibs (if desired), the chopped chocolate, and the cocoa powder mixture. Add the cream (made slightly warm) and the hot melted butter.

4   Preheat the oven to 160°C/320°F. Transfer the batter to the mould, filling it up to 2 cm/¾ in from the top. (Set aside the remaining raw batter.) Bake for 10 minutes, then remove from oven.

5   Use a knife to make a lengthwise cut through the crust. Return to the oven and bake for another 35 minutes. The cake is done when a knife inserted in the centre comes out clean. Un-mould onto a baking rack.

...

6 On a guitar sheet, spread the melted chocolate out into a thin layer using an angled spatula. Refrigerate for a few minutes to harden. Remove and break the chocolate into nice shards.

7 When the cake has cooled, fill the piping bag with the extra raw batter and pipe out a few points to decorate the cake. Place a shard of hardened chocolate atop each dollop of raw batter. Serve.

✤ CHEF'S TIP ✤

For a successful cake batter, make sure to work with ingredients that have been left out at room temperature for at least an hour.

Chocolate-Praline
TART

SERVES 8

PREPARATION TIME: 1 HR 15 – COOKING TIME: 25 MIN – RESTING TIME : 2 HRS

COCOA-FLAVOURED CRUST

200 g/7 oz fine pastry flour (T45) +
  20 g/¾ oz to flour the work surface
120 g/4¼ oz butter + 15 g/½ oz
  to butter the mould
75 g/2½ oz confectioner's (icing) sugar
25 g/⅞ oz powdered almond
12 g/⅓ oz unsweetened cocoa powder
1 egg
A pinch of fleur de sel

CRUNCHY CARAMELIZED ALMOND AND HAZELNUT PRALINE

35 g/1¼ oz milk chocolate
10 g/⅓ oz unsalted butter
150 g/5¼ oz almond-hazelnut praline
60 g/2 oz *crêpes dentelles*

CHOCOLATE GANACHE

300 g/10½ oz dark chocolate (70% cocoa)
300 g/10½ oz heavy (double) cream
100 g/3½ oz butter, room temperature

• • •

COCOA-FLAVOURED CRUST

1 Pass the flour through a sieve into a bowl. Cut the cold butter into small pieces and add to the flour. Add the confectioner's (icing) sugar, powdered almond, cocoa powder, and fleur de sel. Combine with your hands, rubbing the mixture between your palms to obtain a grainy, sandy consistency. Add the egg, mixing just long enough to obtain a homogenous mixture.

2 Roll the dough into a ball and wrap in plastic wrap. Refrigerate for at least 1 hour before using. Flour a work surface, roll the dough out to a thickness of 2 mm. Butter and flour the tart mould, then press the dough into the mould and refrigerate for 1 hour.

3 Preheat the oven to 170°C/338°F. Prick the dough with a fork to prevent it from rising in the oven. Cover with a disc of parchment paper, pressed nicely into the corners of the dough and covered with dry beans. Bake for 25 minutes. Remove from oven and remove the beans and the parchment paper. Allow to cool.

• • •

Praline

EQUIPMENT
Parchment paper
24-cm/9½-in tart mould, 2 cm/
    ¾-inch deep
20-cm/7¾-in tart circle, 2 cm/
    ¾-inch deep
Piping bag fitted with an 8-mm plain tip

CRUNCHY CARAMELIZED ALMOND AND HAZELNUT PRALINE

1 Use a chef's knife to chop the chocolate on a cutting board. Cut the butter into small pieces. Combine the chocolate and butter to melt over a bain-marie, without overheating the mixture. Remove from the bain-marie when melted; the mixture should be lukewarm for the following steps. Stir in the praline and the crumbled *crêpes dentelles*.

2 Place a sheet of parchment paper under the 20-cm pastry circle and spread the mixture out inside with a spatula. Place in the freezer to make it easier to remove the praline for the next steps.

LA GANACHE AU CHOCOLAT

1 Use a chef's knife to finely chop the chocolate, then transfer it to a big bowl. Bring the cream to a boil in a saucepan, then pour half of the boiling cream over the chocolate. Whisk in a circular movement to blend the cream and the chocolate little by little. Add the rest of the hot cream, continuing to whisk in the same fashion.

2 Cut the butter into small pieces and incorporate into the ganache. Use a spatula to stir until the mixture becomes very smooth. Transfer to the piping bag. Begin assembling the tart.

ASSEMBLY

1 Use the piping bag to pipe a thin, 2- to 3-mm layer of ganache out over the crust. Set the disc of crunchy praline over the ganache, pressing down lightly. Finish with a final layer of ganache. Allow to set at room temperature, for 30 minutes. Decorate as desired.

Chocolate-Orange CUPCAKES

SERVES 6

PREPARATION TIME: 35 MIN – COOKING TIME: 20 MIN – RESTING TIME: 24 HRS

CUPCAKE BATTER

160 g/5½ oz unsalted butter

3 eggs

120 g/4¼ oz fine pastry flour (T45)

3 g/ ¹⁄₁₀ oz baking powder

160 g/5½ oz granulated sugar

30 g/1 oz cocoa powder

200 g/7 oz candied orange peel, diced

FILLING

250 g/½ lb fresh orange juice

20 g/¾ oz granulated sugar

A jar of orange marmalade

Chocolate almond paste

CHOCOLATE-ORANGE WHIPPED CREAM

100 g/3½ oz dark chocolate (70% cocoa)

60 g/2 oz whole milk

300 g/10½ oz heavy (double) cream

25 g/⅞ oz granulated sugar

the zest of 2 untreated oranges

CUPCAKE BATTER

1 Set the butter and eggs out at room temperature. Pass the cocoa powder, flour, and baking powder through a sieve into a bowl to combine.

2 In another bowl, beat the room temperature butter into a cream. Add the sugar and whisk vigorously. Whisking continuously, add the eggs one at a time. Using a wooden or silicone spatula, incorporate the cocoa powder mixture. Add the diced candied orange peel.

3 Preheat the oven to 185°C/365°F. Transfer the batter to a piping bag fitted with a plain tip and fill the cupcake moulds up to 2 cm/¾-inch from the top. The cupcakes are done when a knife inserted into the centre comes out clean. Allow to cool.

FILLING

1 Combine the fresh orange juice with the sugar in a small saucepan, and bring to a simmer. Reserve and keep warm.

2 Use a small teaspoon to make a hole in the top of the cupcake, and pour a good spoonful of warm orange juice into the hole. Add a good spoonful of orange marmalade into the hole. Spread a little bit of

• • •

• • •

EQUIPMENT

6 cupcake moulds
Piping bag fitted with a 14-mm plain tip
Piping bag fitted with a 14-mm star tip

chocolate almond paste over the hole, then finish decorating with the Chocolate-Orange Whipped Cream described below.

CHOCOLATE-ORANGE WHIPPED CREAM
The whipped cream must be made the night before and left to rest for 24 hours.

1   Follow the steps for making Chocolate Whipped Cream (see p. 250), then to add a unique touch to your cream, grate the zests of 2 oranges and infuse them in the milk-cream mixture for 20 minutes before chilling.

2   Refrigerate the cream for 24 hours, then whisk into whipped cream. Transfer to a piping bag with a star tip and decorate the cupcakes with a lovely rose. Scatter a few orange zests on top to finish.

Pistachio-Flavoured
HOT CHOCOLATE

MAKES ABOUT 4 CUPS
PREPARATION TIME: 20 MIN

500 g/17½ oz whole milk
90 g/3 oz bittersweet chocolate
  (67% cocoa)
25 g/⅞ oz bittersweet chocolate
  (80% cocoa)
50 g/1½ oz granulated sugar
25 g/⅞ oz natural pistachio paste

EQUIPMENT
Hand blender

1 Combine the milk and sugar together with 75 g/2½ oz of water in a saucepan and bring to a simmer. Cut the chocolate into small pieces.

2 Remove the saucepan from the heat and stir in the chocolate pieces with a whisk. Use a hand blender to mix into a homogenous liquid, then add the natural pistachio paste. Blend again.

3 Transfer to cups and serve immediately.

❖ CHEF'S TIPS ❖
If you like thick hot chocolate, return the saucepan to the heat after adding the pieces of chocolate to the milk, then bring back to a simmer while stirring with the whisk to prevent the chocolate from sticking to the bottom of the saucepan.

TEMPERING CHOCOLATE

In order to obtain a melted chocolate that is fluid and shiny, with no trace of whiteness or marbling, and in order to prevent it from fading, tempering is indispensable. This technique is used to make the coating for chocolate bonbons, brittle, or chocolate decoration.

Tempering chocolate is not very complicated, but does require a bit of organization, dexterity, and a thermometer.

There are two methods for tempering – seeding and tabling – either of which you can use for any of the recipes in this book. Simply choose the method with which you are most at ease.

TEMPERING CHOCOLATE:
The Seeding Method

FOR 600 G/21 OZ CHOCOLATE
PREPARATION TIME: 30 MIN

EQUIPMENT

A chocolate thermometer

1 Fill a pot ⅓ full of water. Heat over a low flame without bringing to a boil. Place a recipient over the pot such that it is in contact with the water, without touching the bottom of the pot.

2 Chop up all of the chocolate with a chef's knife. Melt ⅔ of the chocolate in the recipient, stirring regularly with a spatula.

3 When the chocolate has melted to 45-50°C/113-122°F, remove the recipient from the bain-marie before adding the final ⅓ of untempered chocolate. Stir until the temperature of the chocolate comes back down to 28-29°C/82-84°F for dark chocolate, 27-28°C/80-82°F for milk chocolate, and 26-27°C/79-80°F for white chocolate.

4 Return the recipient to the bain-marie without turning on the heat. Stir gently until the desired temperature is reached for each chocolate: 30-31°C/86-88°F for dark, 28-29°C/82-84°F for milk, 27-28°C/80-82°F for white.

TEMPERING CHOCOLATE:
The Tabling Method

FOR 600 G/21 OZ CHOCOLATE
PREPARATION TIME: 30 MIN

1 Fill a pot ⅓ full of water. Heat over a low flame without bringing to a boil. Place a recipient over the pot such that it is in contact with the water, without touching the bottom of the pot.

2 Chop up all of the chocolate with a chef's knife. Melt all of the chocolate in the recipient, stirring regularly with a spatula.

3 When the chocolate has melted to 45-50°C/113-122°F, remove the recipient from the bain-marie and pour ⅔ of the melted chocolate out onto a marble or stainless-steel work surface. Keep the remaining ⅓ warm. Using the 2 palette knives, spread the chocolate back and forth over the work surface without stopping, until the chocolate reaches the desired temperature: 28-29°C/82-84°F for dark chocolate, 27-28°C/80-82°F for milk chocolate, and 26-27°C/79-80°F for white chocolate.

4 Return the chocolate to the recipient with the remaining ⅓ of melted chocolate without turning on the flame. Stir gently until the desired temperature is reached for each chocolate: 30-31°C/86-88°F for dark, 28-29°C/82-84°F for milk, 27-28°C/80-82°F for white.

EQUIPMENT

A chocolate thermometer
2 palette knives

RECIPE INDEX

ILLUSTRATIONS

Page 11 : © BnF, Dist.RMN-Grand/image BnF ; Paris, Bibliothèque nationale de France (BnF) – Page 15, left: © Album/Oronoz/AKG ; Museo de America-coleccion, Madrid, Espagne – Page 15, right: © Gift of Bonnie and David Ross/ The Bridgeman Art Library ; Indianapolis Museum of Art, USA – Page 17 : © Akg-images ; SPSG – Page 19, left: © Muséum national d'Histoire naturelle, Dist. RMN-Grand Palais/image du MNHN, bibliothèque centrale ; Paris, Muséum national d'Histoire naturelle, bibliothèque centrale – Page 19, right: © Muséum national d'Histoire naturelle, Dist. RMN-Grand Palais/image du MNHN, bibliothèque centrale ; Paris, Muséum national d'Histoire naturelle, bibliothèque centrale – Page 20 : © Muséum national d'Histoire naturelle, Dist. RMN-Grand Palais/image du MNHN, bibliothèque centrale ; Paris, Muséum national d'Histoire naturelle, bibliothèque centrale – Page 21 : © Florilegius/ Leemage ; Private Collection – Page 22 : © Heritage Images / Leemage – Page 23 : © Photo Josse / Leemage ; Private Collection – Page 24 : © Akg-images – Page 26 : © Akg-images – Page 27 : © Gift of the Lowe Art Museum, University of Miami/Gift of Toby and Robert Stoetzer/ The Bridgeman Art Library ; Collection of the Lowe Art Museum, University of Miami – Page 29 : © Akg-images ; Bibliothèque Nationale – Page 30 : © Prado, Madrid, Spain/Giraudon/ The Bridgeman Art Library ; Prado, Madrid, Spain – Page 32, left: © Collection Kharbine-Tapabor – Page 32, centre: © Collection Kharbine-Tapabor – Page 32, right: © Collection Kharbine-Tapabor – Page 35 : © Photo Josse/Leemage ; Tate gallery, Londres – Pages 38-39 : © Photo Josse/Leemage ; Musée du Nouveau Monde, La Rochelle –

Page 42, left: © Heritage Images/Leemage ; Oxford Science Archive – Page 42, right: © Collection Kharbine-Tapabor – Page 45 : © Akg-images – Page 47 : © RMN-Grand Palais (Sèvres, cité de la céramique)/Martine ; Manufacture de Sèvres – Page 50 : © Photo Josse/Leemage – Page 53 : © Bianchetti/ Leemage ; Private Collection – Page 54 : Musée de l'Impression sur Étoffes, Mulhouse – Page 56 : © Collection Kharbine-Tapabor – Page 60 : © Alinari/The Bridgeman Art Library ; Museo Civico di Storia ed Arte, Modena, Italy – Page 57 : Musée de l'Impression sur Étoffes, Mulhouse – Page 63 : © RMN-Grand Palais (château de Versailles)/Gérard Blot ; Versailles, château de Versailles et de Trianon – Page 67, left: © RMN-Grand Palais (musée du Louvre)/Jean-Gilles Berizzi ; Paris, musée du Louvre – Page 67, right: © Collection Kharbine-Tapabor – Page 69, top left: © RMN-Grand Palais (Limoges, Cité de la céramique)/Jean-Gilles Berizzi ; Limoges, musée Adrien Dubouché – Page 69, top centre: © RMN-Grand Palais (Limoges, Cité de la céramique)/Jean-Gilles Berizzi ; Limoges, musée Adrien Dubouché – Page 69, top right: © RMN-Grand Palais (Limoges, Cité de la céramique)/Jean-Gilles Berizzi ; Limoges, musée Adrien Dubouché – Page 69, second row left: © RMN-Grand Palais (Limoges, Cité de la céramique)/Jean-Gilles Berizzi ; Limoges, musée Adrien Dubouché – Page 69, second row centre: © RMN-Grand Palais (Limoges, Cité de la céramique)/Jean-Gilles Berizzi ; Limoges, musée Adrien Dubouché – Page 69, second row right: © RMN-Grand Palais (Limoges, Cité de la céramique)/ Jean-Gilles Berizzi ; Limoges, musée Adrien Dubouché – Page 69, third row left: © RMN-Grand Palais (Limoges, Cité de la céramique)/Jean-Gilles Berizzi ; Limoges, musée Adrien Dubouché –

ACKNOWLEDGEMENTS

La Maison Ladurée is infinitely thankful to all of its teams, especially to Julien Christophe and Vincent Lemains for their recipes and creations, Antoine Bled (Vincent Lemains's right hand), Mickael Gandon (Julien Christophe's right hand), and the department of Marketing and Communication.

Serge Gleizes would like to thank Valerie Winckler.

Noëlle Hoeppe and Nelson Sepulveda-Osorio would like to thank Bernardaud, Fedrigoni, Laurence Brabant, Le Bon Marché, Raynaud, Surface and The Conran Shop for lending a stylistic touch to their photographs.

JULIEN CHRISTOPHE
Head of Chocolate Production

VINCENT LEMAINS
Head of Pastry Creation

Now the head chocolatier at the *Marquis de Ladurée*, this passionate, talented young chef has been with Ladurée for the past eleven years. Since 2007, he has been head of creation and all chocolate-making processes at Ladurée's chocolate laboratory.

Leading a team of 10 people, he created the entire collection of chocolates, taking inspiration from the history of the company and the symbols of the brand.

Julien Christophe enjoys making new discoveries, while maintaining a certain classical approach; steeped in tradition, he takes pleasure in using fresh, seasonal products.

Several times a year, he showcases special creations to mark the year's important moments, like Christmas, Easter, and Valentine's Day.

Vincent Lemains has been head of pastry creation at Ladurée since 2010. This young chef learned an appreciation for fine work, technique, the quality of basic ingredients, and rigour under the wing of the great Chef Alain Ducasse.

In the past four years, he has proven his worth, advancing through all of the stages required to rise in our company. Today, he is responsible for all of Ladurée's beautiful pastry creations, like the *Fraise*, the *Butterfly*, the *Corolle* …

Working closely for several months with our Head Chocolatier, he lovingly conceived all of the pastry creations for our new collection, *Les Marquis*.

Published in the UK by **Scriptum Editions**, 2014
An imprint of **Co & Bear Productions (UK) Ltd**
www.scriptumeditions.co.uk

Publishers: Beatrice Vincenzini & Francesco Venturi

First Edition
2 4 6 8 10 9 7 5 3 1

Distributed by Thames & Hudson

ISBN: 978–1–902686–80-6

First published in French by Éditions du Chêne, 2013
© Éditions du Chêne – Hachette Livre, 2013
Managing Editor: Valérie Tognali
Assistant Editor: Françoise Mathay
Translation from French: Lyn Thompson Lemaire
Art Director: Sabine Houplain assisted by
Claire Mieyeville and Audrey Lorel
Design and Layout: Laura Yates
English layout: Vincent Lanceau aided by Mister Cat

Printed in China